# CREATING A SAFE CAMPUS

## ABOUT THE AUTHOR

David Nichols is the Director of Public Safety at Jacksonville State University and teaches part-time in the College of Criminal Justice there. He is a veteran law enforcement professional having served as chief of police at three universities. His law enforcement experience spans eighteen years and includes work with municipal, county, and campus agencies.

He holds a Doctor of Education degree with a major in Administration of Higher Education from the University of Alabama. He received a Master's degree in School Administration and a Bachelor's degree in Political Science from the University of Montevallo. He also has a graduate concentration in criminal justice from Jacksonville State University and the University of Virginia. He is a graduate of the prestigious FBI National Academy.

Nichols has published widely in the area of law enforcement and security. He is the author of two books, *The Administration of Public Safety In Higher Education* and *University-Community Relations: Living Together Effectively.* He has published more than eighteen articles and reviews in such noted journals as the *FBI Law Enforcement Bulletin, The Police Chief, Journal of Higher Education,* and the *National Association of Secondary School Principals Journal.* He has been quoted in several national publications to include the *Chronicle of Higher Education* and *Money* magazine.

In addition to his significant accomplishments as a police administrator, Nichols serves as a law enforcement consultant to both university and municipal police agencies. He has been an expert witness in several cases related to campus security. He has assisted public school officials in developing safety and security procedures. A former public school teacher, he currently serves on the Jacksonville City Board of Education. He has distinguished himself as a guest speaker, lecturer, and workshop presenter for professional associations and police groups.

# CREATING A SAFE CAMPUS

## A Guide For College and University Administrators

*By*

**DAVID NICHOLS, ED.D.**

*Jacksonville State University*
*Jacksonville, Alabama*

CHARLES C THOMAS • PUBLISHER, LTD.
*Springfield • Illinois • U.S.A.*

*Published and Distributed Throughout the World by*

CHARLES C THOMAS • PUBLISHER, LTD.
2600 South First Street
Springfield, Illinois 62794-9265

© *1997 by* CHARLES C THOMAS • PUBLISHER, LTD.
ISBN 0-398-06727-9 (cloth)
ISBN 0-398-06728-7 (paper)
Library of Congress Catalog Card Number: 96-35578

*With* THOMAS BOOKS *careful attention is given to all details of manufacturing
and design. It is the Publisher's desire to present books that are satisfactory as to
their physical qualities and artistic possibilities and appropriate for their particular
use.* THOMAS BOOKS *will be true to those laws of quality that assure a good
name and good will.*

*Printed in the United States of America*
*SC-R-3*

**Library of Congress Cataloging-in-Publication Data**

Nichols, David, Ed. D.
    Creating a safe campus : a guide for college and university
administrators / by David Nichols.
        p.    cm.
    Includes index.
    ISBN 0-398-06709-0 (cloth). — ISBN 0-398-06710-4 (paper)
    1. Universities and colleges—Security measures—United States.
2. College students—Crimes against—United States—Prevention.
I. Title.
LB2866.N54   1997
378.1'88—dc20                                                                        96-35578
                                                                                           CIP

# PREFACE

Higher education officials understand the significance of a positive and attractive campus environment in which their students can pursue their academic, social, and personal goals. They also appreciate the image projected by a pleasant campus and the impact that can have on prospective students, parents, alumni, board members, and the public. Recognizing that the perceptions of these constituencies are critical to the institution, assiduous college and university administrators know the importance of creating a safe campus.

Crime and violence have intruded our campuses. Once considered sanctuaries from the outside influences of criminals and perpetrators of evil doings, today many campuses reflect the ills of our society. As the crime rate in the United States has dramatically escalated in the past decade, so has fear and anxiety among everyday Americans. These concerns are especially shared by the mothers and fathers who send their children off to college only to be inundated with media reports which depict college campuses as danger zones where students are murdered, raped, and robbed at will. While few of our nation's campuses are actually ravaged by crime and violence, the issue of safety on campus has become a critical one for students, parents, and higher education officials. In fact, campus crime was raised to a national awareness level as evidenced by the passage by Congress of the Campus Security Act of 1990, a significant law requiring colleges and universities to report crime and develop better security programs. Issues of liability, negligence, duty of care and other legal matters relating to student safety also gained the attention of both public and private university officials.

While some campus administrators have moved to comply with legal mandates and to enhance security measures, many officials have not yet developed a broad-based, comprehensive approach to creating a safe campus. Consequently, they continue to deal with recurring problems of crime, violence, and a wide array of misconduct which diminish campus life and create a serious perception dilemma for the institution. The first three chapters of this volume are designed to offer college and university officials a realistic view of today's campus environment. They also present issues and threats which impact the campus community and its students. The remaining seven chapters offer practical recommendations which are presented in terms of critical components for creating a safe campus. These seven critical components are: (1) effective student affairs; (2) effective police and security services; (3) community policing; (4) secure campus housing; (5) physical/environmental security; (6) records, reporting, and disclosure; and (7) a collaborative approach. Perhaps the common denominator in accomplishing this is the idea of a campus-wide, shared responsibility. Reducing crime and the risks associated with violence, disorders, and misconduct is not just a police or security concern, but rather it should be a collaborative effort.

This book should assist student affairs professionals, campus judicial officers, housing personnel, campus police/security officials, faculty, and university administrators, whatever their titles, in their concerted efforts to create a safe campus. It is written for campus officials at varying types and sizes of institutions to include public or private, urban or rural, four-year or two-year, commuter or residential, liberal arts or technical, professional or undergraduate, and small or large. I hope that this book will contribute to the recognition and acceptance of sound principles and practices that will enhance the quality of life on our campuses across the nation.

# ACKNOWLEDGMENTS

I am especially indebted to my wife, Teresa Nichols, who encouraged me with the idea for this volume and supported my efforts throughout the research and writing. My children, Jarrod and Brooke, always expressed their support and pride for their Dad during the many hours I spent isolated from their activities. I am grateful to Tom Barker, Dean of the College of Criminal Justice at Jacksonville State University, for his guidance and advice which contributed to ideas and improvements in this effort. As always, I am appreciative to my secretary, Shelia Newell, for the many hours she devoted in preparing the manuscript. And finally, a word of gratitude is due to administration officials at Jacksonville State University for allowing me the time and giving me the support necessary to accomplish such an extensive research and writing endeavor.

# CONTENTS

             *Page*

*Preface* . . . . . . . . . . . . . . . . . . . . . . . . . . . . . . . . . . . . . . . . . . . . . . . . . . . v

*Chapter*

  1. The College Campus in Transition . . . . . . . . . . . . . . . . . . . . 3
  2. Issues and Impacts of Campus Crime . . . . . . . . . . . . . . . . . 12
  3. Threats To a Safe Campus . . . . . . . . . . . . . . . . . . . . . . . . . 27
  4. Effective Student Affairs . . . . . . . . . . . . . . . . . . . . . . . . . . 48
  5. Effective Police and Security Services . . . . . . . . . . . . . . . . 66
  6. Community Policing on Campus . . . . . . . . . . . . . . . . . . . . . 83
  7. Secure Campus Housing . . . . . . . . . . . . . . . . . . . . . . . . . 103
  8. Physical/Environmental Security . . . . . . . . . . . . . . . . . . . 124
  9. Records, Reporting, and Disclosure . . . . . . . . . . . . . . . . . 140
 10. A Collaborative Approach . . . . . . . . . . . . . . . . . . . . . . . . 153
      *Index* . . . . . . . . . . . . . . . . . . . . . . . . . . . . . . . . . . . . . . 173

# CREATING A SAFE CAMPUS

# Chapter 1

# THE COLLEGE CAMPUS IN TRANSITION

## THE EARLY YEARS

Higher education institutions in America have fostered enormous changes and have influenced our society's social, political, and economic transformation for more than three centuries. Colleges and universities have made significant contributions to a growing nation through research, service, and teaching. Scientific breakthroughs, technological advancements, cultural enrichment, and educational improvements are all direct impacts of higher education. In turn, colleges and universities with their varied missions and goals have been constrained, propagated, and molded by political officials, government programs, the national economy, and a constantly changing political/social agenda. These postsecondary institutions have, at times, endured the impacts of an insufficient national wealth, world wars, depression, inflation, political upheaval, and social convulsions. At other times they have been the recipients of huge federally funded programs, legislative mandates, philanthropic contributions, record enrollments, and burgeoning economies. To some extent it can be said that America's higher education institutions and the nation with its political/social/economic nature have a reciprocal relationship. In many ways colleges and universities often mirror society's health, wealth, and national agenda.

This is of particular significance when examining environmental aspects of the college campus. This was true as far back as the late 1600s when colonial college officials labored to replicate the elaborate quadrangular dormitories found in Oxford and Cambridge. They felt that these living arrangements would create a special intellectual and social atmosphere. However, due to an insufficient national wealth and little or no government support, these early American colleges' "barracks-like dormitories were not designed to foster the characteristics of a close and well-knit social life . . ."[1].

Today's colleges and universities also experience the impacts of our nation's political and economic agendas. Even in the mid-1990s, nearly three centuries removed from the colonial colleges, colleges and universities face financial aid cut-backs and an increasing austere national economy which threaten academic programs.[2]

The issue of campus crime, violence, and student misconduct offers a poignant example of how campus environments reflect the mood and conditions of society at large. In the early years of American higher education, college campuses were generally tranquil communities where little real crime occurred. Minor infractions and violations were usually the responsibility of faculty members.[3] Much like American society during those years, some upheaval did occasionally occur. During the early 1800s, a few isolated student riots, disruptions, and brawls were reported on several American college campuses. In 1807, at Princeton more than half of the student body was suspended for a violent rebellion. The usually quiet campus of Harvard was disrupted by a brawl in 1820 and in 1834 experienced a student riot. In 1841, town-versus-gown confrontations occurred between Yale students and local New Haven firemen.[4]

These incidents simply mirrored similar conditions of a growing nation. During this same period the most common complaints received by town constables and local police were minor misconduct, i.e., disorderly conduct, drunkenness, and fighting. Like the college campuses of this era, a few isolated towns and cities experienced riots—some minor and some disastrous. For example, as early as 1805 constables in Charleston, South Carolina were authorized by city ordinances to control "tumultuous riots."[5] Sometime later in 1863 the bloodiest riot in United States history occurred in New York City (1,200 people killed and 8,000 injured!)[6] Despite these uncommon incidents, street crime and random violence in America did not reach the proportions of modern day crime rates. Crime was certainly not on the national agenda of issues of concern to Americans. These preindustrial years were marked by a rural, agrarian society which found little need of police forces, especially in small towns and cities, until the mid-1800s. Campuses similarly had little real crime and no need for security forces or police. They remained generally idyllic settings reserved for a relative small number of elite who could afford the luxury of higher education.

## INFLUENCES OF CHANGE

A century later, the picture changed significantly across the country and on many of our nation's campuses. Several major factors came together just prior to and during the 1960s which transformed higher education since colonial times to a multi-billion dollar industry it is today. These factors included increased enrollments, increased endowments, the Vietnam War, the Civil Rights movement, the popularity of recreational drug use, a social revolution, and program adaptations for nontraditional students. Perhaps the single most influential impact on higher education was federal funding. The National Defense Education Act of 1958 provided millions of dollars in student loans to undergraduates, graduate fellowships, and subsidies to university-based teacher-training programs. By 1960, the federal government was spending for research programs alone over $750,000,000 a year in educational institutions and allied research centers. By 1962, over two billion dollars had been loaned through the Housing and Home Financing Agency to colleges and universities (public and private) to build dormitories and other revenue-producing facilities. The Higher Education Act of 1965 was the first federal measure to provide a broad permanent program of financial aid to both public and private colleges as well as to individual college students. This omnibus act provided millions of dollars to higher education institutions to solve community problems, improve and expand libraries, and to raise the quality of academic programs.[7] America moved rapidly from a few small colleges serving the wealthy and socially elite to the world's most egalitarian system of higher education.

## ENVIRONMENTAL IMPACTS

These tremendous impacts on American higher education also caused a dramatic environmental change to the campus. Increased enrollments coupled with a more diverse student population created a different social atmosphere. Political and cultural issues—the civil rights movement, drugs, the draft and Vietnam War protests—became rallying points for many students. As in the nineteenth century, the 1960s reflect parallels with the campus climate and that of American society. In both the South and North, civil rights demonstrations brought protestors into direct confrontation with the police. The frustration of African-Americans finally exploded into violent disorders in 1964. Riots broke out in Los

Angeles, Newark, Detroit, and New York City.[8] In his book, *Coping With Crime On Campus,* Michael Clay Smith observes:

> In a physical sense, the privileged sanctuary status of the campus began to diminish in the post-World War II period. . . . With the wall between academe and the world outside disintegrating, inevitably the problems of the larger cultures have begun to intrude upon the academy.[9]

## STUDENT ACTIVISM

Student activism in the sixties was not only directed at national issues such as Vietnam, the draft, and civil rights, but also sometimes more specifically toward university policies and officials. In 1964, the University of California at Berkeley student activists brought the direct confrontation tactics and nonviolent ideology of the civil rights movement onto the American campus under the guise of the Free Speech Movement. The activists' aim in 1964 was to create a sociological climate in which discussion and democratic participation became meaningless so that they might advance their own causes and obtain direct access to power. These students questioned the legitimacy of the entire political process — on and off campus. They addressed such issues as the Vietnam War, the draft, problems of poverty and urban blight, university complicity in military research and recruitment, ethnic studies, and even the "credibility gap."[10] The Berkeley movement also represented, to some extent, a new generation of college students during the sixties which rejected the traditional notion of *in loco parentis* which implied that they needed nurture and care through their college years. Berkeley was by no means the only campus in crisis. The student takeover and occupation of campus buildings at Columbia University in the Spring of 1968 ended with the bloody clash with the New York City Police.[11] Toward the end of this student protest era was, perhaps, the worst incident of all. National Guardsmen firing into a crowd of students at Kent State University killed four and wounded nine.[12]

In retrospect, the decade 1960–70 seemed to fall short of the expectations of many students. A number of former activists felt that little or nothing had been accomplished.[13] The radical movement seemed to fade almost as suddenly as it was born. Yet, it changed forever the face of the campus in a unique way. For the first time in history, disorder and intentional lawbreaking became a national phenomenon on America's college campuses. Local and state police and even state militia had become a new sight within the walls of ivy and halls of academe. Campus police departments had become an added line item in most university budgets to achieve calm. While the sit-ins and protests ended with the sixties, the campus community would soon face a new societal ill—crime.

## GROWTH IN THE HIGHER EDUCATION ENTERPRISE

If a modern-day Rip Van Winkle had fallen asleep in 1970 and awakened twenty years later, he would discover a significantly changed campus environment at many institutions of higher education. Following two decades of growth, prosperity and change, higher education in America is dramatically different in several ways. First, enrollment has risen significantly. According to the American Council on Education, in 1968, 6,928,000 students were enrolled in postsecondary institutions.[14] By the Fall of 1992, that number had climbed to more than 14,000,000—doubled in twenty-four years.[15] This appears to be a particularly radical change in view of the fact that during this same time period the country's population increased only about ten percent. Second, the number of institutions has increased. In 1955, a total of 1,855 American colleges and universities were in operation.[16] By 1994, there were 3,600 accredited colleges and universities.[17] Third, most campuses are more culturally and racially diverse. Minority enrollments have steadily risen. According to the U.S. Department of Education, numbers and percentages of African, and Hispanic students increased from 1982 to 1992.[18] Fourth, technology and communications has transformed many processes and programs on today's campus. It is the age of on-line college admissions, of cyberspace conferences, of electronic journals, of computerized models of the human body, and of remote classrooms linked by two-way video connections. It is the age of the Internet. The explosive growth of technology is expected to continue. Fifth, the campus environment itself is considerably different than it was in 1960. Most campuses are more accessible and open to vehicular traffic—both students and nonstudents. In some instances as institutions have experienced tremendous growth, surrounding neighborhoods have deteriorated. In other cases, once small urban colleges are now large, downtown institutions in cities that have seen once-thriving businesses and residents move to the suburbs. Some residential institutions have experienced a decline in on-campus occupancy for preference to nearby off-campus apartments. The campus community is more often confronted by a whole new set of issues which will be addressed later in this chapter.

## HIGHER EDUCATION IN A CHANGING SOCIETY

As the 21st century approaches, academic institutions face dramatic societal changes which will impact policies, programs, expansion, and funding strategies. Colleges and universities must respond to a variety of challenges to their cultural heritage. For example, there is a gradual substantive change in the reticence on the part of academic leadership and faculty to recognize the importance of undergraduate students as the primary customers of most of this country's academic institutions.

Major societal changes demand that higher education leaders develop strategies which will enable their institutions to remain in business and to be more competitive. There are several societal factors that would seriously affect colleges and universities in the 1990s. They are:

> Increased demand for a higher level of educational attainment from workers,
>
> Major dislocations in the workforce due to downsizing, and the emergence of flatter network organizations,
>
> Increasing mobility of the workforce and multiple career changes,
>
> Fierce international competition for market share and productivity gains, and
>
> Advances in technology and communications and a change in the concepts of work and education.[19]

America's colleges and universities are experiencing major financial problems leading to large budget deficits and erosion of financial reserves. Many institutions have had a significant loss in student enrollments or an increasing need to discount tuition to recruit new students. Federal and state tax initiatives have reduced the flow of revenues to some institutions. Some state government fiscal austerity measures have directly impacted higher education institutions.

The current economic and political environment has put a choke hold on the financial situation of most colleges and universities. Government revenue sources are being redirected to other competing societal programs such as welfare, public health, elementary and secondary education, and criminal justice. Tax increases are, and will continue to be, political anathemas. Finally, the low rate of inflation and intense competition for students limit the ability to pass on significant tuition increases.

Higher education officials are also beginning to realize that students are customers. With the average age of the student population increasing, older students share more specific educational goals and are more articulate in describing their expectations. They are less inclined to accept poor teaching or ineffective administrative services. Students also realize that institutions suffering low enrollment levels are more likely to anticipate and be responsive to their needs.[20]

## CRIME AND VIOLENCE 101: ISSUES 2000

Along with the Internet, big time college sports, and new technology curricula comes "Crime and Violence 101" to our college campuses. Crime, while not a totally new visitor to the college campus, represents a societal influence on higher education institutions across the country. As college and university administrators and faculty strive to meet the challenges of and needs of a society in transition, they find themselves forced to deal with the unpleasant, "unacademic" issue of crime. They find themselves faced with expectations of parents, students, and the public that their campuses must be immune to crime. They find themselves faced with the reality that their campuses are no longer sanctuaries apart from society with all of its ills. Campus crime, violence, student misconduct and associated problems are issues which have serious and long-term impacts on our institutions of higher education. Heretofore, many college and university officials who have, by and large, ignored those issues and impacts now recognize the significance of addressing them with effective strategies. Contemporary higher education administrators should understand the importance of creating a safe campus.

Virtually every aspect of campus life today must be assessed in terms of safety and security considerations. Safety in campus access, class attendance, social activities, athletic events, and residence life has become a critical issue for campus officials who have witnessed increased threats to their traditionally safe campus environs. Assaults, rapes, robberies, and burglaries plague the sanctuaries of higher learning. Alcohol and drug abuse, guns, hazing, racial tensions, and carjackings are also escalating crime-related issues to which college and university administrators must respond.

## SUMMARY

The transition of American higher education since its inception has been phenomenal. As America has moved from a small agrarian society through the industrial revolution to the information age, colleges and universities have adapted their roles, expanded their curricula, and provided research and technology to fuel the growth of the national economy.

The college campus itself has been forever changed by the influences of an expanding nation. American political, social, and economic issues have impacted virtually every college and university campus in the country. The national agenda issues have also, in fact, resulted in the expansion of existing higher education institutions and a proliferation of new colleges and universities across the country. Federal dollars, social changes, and a growing population have made higher education a big business. Their residence populations reach into the thousands, their retail businesses are thriving, their recruiting and marketing efforts are impressive, and their customer-driven economics are competitive.

The campus community's climate has become transformed as a result of society's changes. The tranquil campus of the nineteenth and early twentieth centuries has often become one of a bustling, traffic congested streets, crowded residence halls and wild parties. Major sporting events can transform the usual campus climate into a spirited environ of more than one hundred thousand frenzied fans. Campuses originally designed and constructed for no or few automobiles have become inundated with expansive parking lots and multifloor parking decks.

Finally, one of American society's most regrettable changes, crime, has not spared its impact on our nation's college campuses. Threats to a safe campus have resulted in numerous adaptive programs and responses. Police, once foreign to the hallowed halls of academe, have become an expected budget line item at most colleges and universities. Fences, sophisticated security systems, police cruisers, and metal detectors can be found on today's college campus. Special programming to educate students about safety and self-protection are seen as requirements. Student activities now call for extensive security planning, special restrictions, and armed guards. Like it or not, contemporary college and university administrators must recognize that the transition of the college campus and all that has evolved from it, now calls for leadership that places a safe campus high on the institution's priority of goals and objectives. Creating a safe campus with a zero-tolerance approach to crime and violence should become a fundamental philosophy among all higher education officials.

## ENDNOTES

1. John S. Brubacher and Willis Rudy, *Higher Education in Transition,* 3rd ed. (New York: Harper & Row, 1976), p. 41.
2. Scott Jaschik, "Defense Budget Approved By House Would Halve President's Request for University Research", *The Chronicle of Higher Education,* Volume XL, Number 44, July 6, 1994, p. A31.
3. Brubacher and Rudy, p. 42.
4. Michael Clay Smith, *Coping With Crime On Campus,* (New York: MacMillan Publishing Company, 1988), pp. 6 & 7.
5. Richard N. Holden, *Law Enforcement: An Introduction,* (New Jersey: Prentice-Hall, 1992), p. 57.
6. Holden, p. 59.
7. Brubacher and Rudy, pp. 232–236.
8. Samuel Walker, *The Police In America* (New York: McGraw-Hill, 1983), pp. 22 & 23.
9. Smith, p. 8.
10. G. Louis Heath, *The Hot Campus: The Politics That Impede Change in the Technoversity* (New Jersey: The Scarecrow Press, Inc., 1973), pp. 16–21.
11. Walker, p. 22.
12. Smith, p. 9.
13. Brubacher and Rudy, p. 353.
14. Ibid, p. 400.
15. *The Chronicle of Higher Education: Almanac Issue,* Vol. XLI, No. 1, September 1, 1994, p. 14.
16. Brubacher and Rudy, p. 406.
17. Jean Evangelauf, "A New Carnegie Classification", *The Chronicle of Higher Education,* Vol. XL, No. 31, April 6, 1994, p. A17.
18. The Chronicle: Almanac, p. 15.
19. K. Scott Hughes, "Transforming Academic Institutions", *NACUBO Business Officer,* August, 1995, pp. 1–3.
20. Ibid.

# Chapter 2

# ISSUES AND IMPACTS OF CAMPUS CRIME

## INTRODUCTION

Academe is a big business which depends on a positive image, plenty of customers, and large amounts of money. Higher education officials increasingly recognize the "crunch" to compete during economically austere years in which federal dollars to colleges and universities are being diverted to crime control and deficit reduction, where state funding levels to higher education are in jeopardy, and where endowments and foundation monies are being used up at higher rates than contributions. Add to this the dwindling pool of high school graduates and an increasing number of colleges and universities competing for the same students.[1] College administrators are keenly aware of the importance of becoming more "customer friendly" and ensuring that their institutions remain fiscally healthy and are attractive to prospective students as well as their parents.

Efforts to achieve a competitive edge and, sometimes, just to stay "afloat" financially often include such strategies as intercollegiate consortia, fundraising/development programs, ongoing grant writing projects, high-tech recruiting programs, and comprehensive retention activities. Certainly these are among successful efforts used by many colleges and universities. Yet, despite these successes officials at institutions across the country have discovered that incidents of serious crime can significantly tarnish a positive image and negate years of progress. When campus crime and violence strikes, the toll on the institution may be immediately devastating and have long-term impacts on recruiting, financial support, and public image. One institution hit hard by crime and violence is Johns Hopkins where faculty, staff, and students complained about security at the east Baltimore campus. In an effort to calm fears and reduce incidents of violence, university officials overhauled the $7 million security operation. One university official there expressed it this way: "We're stepping up security because the increasing crime is taking away from Hopkin's ability to attract the best people."[2]

It is incumbent on higher education chief executive officers to recognize that crime, violence, and the concomitant perceptions of threat are critical issues which must be addressed. Creating a safe campus should be an essential component among strategies to achieve institutional goals, attract the "best people", and sustain a climate where academic and social growth can occur.

Until recently, many college and university officials managed to avoid the negative impacts of crime and violence by simply not reporting it to students, the media, the public, or any official clearing house. The reluctance by these officials to admit criminal incidents did exist, perpetuated the myth that their institutions were sanctuaries immune to crime. These "cover-ups" have been made more difficult with the passage of the federal Crime Awareness and Campus Security Act of 1990. Its passage was the culmination of years of emotionally charged efforts of Howard and Constance Cleary whose daughter was brutally murdered on the campus of Lehigh University in Pennsylvania. The Act requires that all postsecondary institutions participating in federal student aid programs to disclose security policies and crime statistics. The provisions of the Act extends reporting requirements of institutions beyond the campus boundaries to off-campus student organizations. Under this Act campus officials are now reporting specified criminal incidents and arrests to the U.S. Department of Education and, in most instances, these crime statistics are open records to the media and public. Consequently, college presidents and other officials should recognize the significant impact crime can have on their institution.

Campus crime impacts virtually all of the university's constituencies from faculty to alumni. Perhaps the group most profoundly affected is students. Students who become victims or even perceive a threat of harm may not remain in school and/or may also become the institution's worst public relations ambassadors. Students who know or believe the campus is unsafe will likely relate this belief to their parents. Faculty members are also victims of all sorts of campus crime, violence, and threats. Faculty morale and confidence in institutional governance can have a detrimental impact on the administration's leadership ability. State higher education governing boards, boards of trustees, or system-wide regulatory agencies also represent concerned constituencies. Certainly, campus crime and violence impacts student affairs personnel, campus police/security, university councils, counselors, student health officials, housing officials and other university administrators and staff.

The scope and significance of campus crimes depends, of course, on the nature and extent of the incidents. When major incidents occur (i.e., homicide in residence hall, race-related riot, or a series of stranger rapes), the impacts can be far-reaching. Such incidents can create panic and fear among students, parents, and faculty. Media coverage usually heightens these fears and often results in unconfirmed rumors. Occupancy in residence halls may decline if incidents occurred in or around a residence hall. Reports and negative publicity of incidents may dissuade some parents of prospective students from sending their children to the institution. Philanthropic contributions could suffer if it is perceived that officials did not respond appropriately. Governing officials such as trustees may scrutinize the president's leadership and ability. The competence of campus police and the quality of security measures will likely be questioned. And finally, recruitment efforts will likely be affected to some extent.

There are, indeed, important issues and impacts that crime brings to bear on colleges and universities. Once higher education officials become familiar with these issues and impacts, understand who is impacted, and recognize the potential significance of the impacts they will be in a position to respond with effective strategies to reduce the risks and repercussions.

## MYTHS AND REALITIES ABOUT CAMPUS CRIME

It is important to recognize several widely-held myths about campus crime and examine the realities of this issue. There are generally two perceptions about campus crime. These perceptions are, in fact, myths. The first myth is that campus crime is rampant and that it is dangerous to walk across a college campus. The second myth holds that there is no crime on campus and that today's college campus is much like the campus of our parents and grandparents—tranquil and completely immune from crime and violence.

So what is the truth or reality about campus crime? Actually, there are several realities that should be examined in order to gain a people perspective about campus crime. The first of these is the reality that there is, in fact, crime on most college campuses. In their first year of compliance to the Right to Know and Campus Security Act, college and university officials reported 30 murders. The 2,400 institutions surveyed also reported a total of 7,500 violent crimes during the 1992–93 academic year.[3] While the figure of 30 murders reported from among 2,400 institutions may appear insignificant, the very occurrence of homicidal behavior on a college campus is seen as a frightening signal that society's ills have spilled onto campus. Crimes of violence are not found to be committed only on the campuses of large urban universities. Few states and few institutions have escaped the menace of some violent incident.

The second reality that, at this time, the significant and rate of campus crime is unclear and often confusing. Currently, only about 15 percent of our nation's 3,600 institutions of higher education report to the U.S. Justice Department's Uniform Crime Reporting (UCR) System. While the UCR's basis for determining the crime rate among counties and municipalities is based on population (incidents per 100,000 inhabitants), campus populations and other demographics are much more ambiguous since enrollments do not equate with residential population. Further, the Crime Awareness and Campus Security Act which mandates that all colleges and universities report specified crimes has not yet proven to be consistent and accurate. There are broad and different interpretations of the Act's requirements, institutional internal reporting processes are not effective, and several categories of the most common campus crimes are not required for reporting to the U.S. Department of Education. Consequently, we actually do not have a real grasp on the extent and rate of campus crime and it is impossible to make any accurate comparisons between institutions.

The third reality is that, despite some reports, serious campus crime is not rampant. In fact, most reported campus crime is comprised of larceny/theft, property crime, and public order crime (disorderly conduct, drunkenness, etc.). Incidents of serious crimes such as murder, rape, robbery and aggravated assault are relatively infrequent and almost nonexistent on many campuses such as small rural colleges and two-year commuter colleges. While the Campus Security Act does not require reporting of these crimes, both campus security officials and researchers on the topic report that these less serious crimes more commonly occur on most campuses.[4] One research study reported that property crime makes up nearly 98 percent of all campus crime.[5]

The fourth reality is that contrary to the perceptions and assumptions by some, most campus crime is perpetrated by students against other students. The findings of Congress presented in the Campus Security

Act state that according to reports from "National Campus Violence Surveys" roughly 80 percent of campus crimes are committed by a student upon another student.[6] An extensive study conducted by the Center for the Study of Campus Violence at Maryland's Towson State University indicated that 78 percent of campus sexual assaults, 82 percent of other assaults, 86 percent of campus vandalism, and 92 percent of arson incidents were committed by students.[7] However, all indications are that the majority of crimes occurring on most campuses are nonviolent misdemeanors such as theft in residence halls and disorderly conduct at social events where students are interacting and living communally. Few of our campuses are under siege from outside intruders. In fact, in many of those more serious crimes such as murder and date rape, both the victims and perpetrators are students. This is not to diminish the issues and problems of criminal behavior but does offer some perspective to the nature and extent of those involved so that appropriate preventive strategies can be developed.

The fifth reality about campus crime is that its occurrence is a reflection of crime in our country. While campus crime rates are unknown and cannot be compared to those of local jurisdictions, there are some striking similarities (the nature of crime on campus and its rise and fall) to crime in America. This concept was previously discussed in this chapter with regard to earlier periods of American history. Violence in America continues to rise. According to the U.S. Justice Department's Uniform Crime Reports (1993) violent crime increased by 17 percent from 1989 to 1993. A major concern is that the use of firearms in violent crimes increased from 27 percent in 1989 to 32 percent in 1993. The report presents another alarming phenomenon. Prior to 1990 over one half of murder victims knew their killers. That has shifted down to 47 percent in 1993 and clearly indicates what many had feared—that murder and other violence is more random. Firearms is increasingly becoming the weapon of choice with seven out of every ten murders in 1993 committed with firearms.[8] Likewise, reported crime on university and college campuses has increased dramatically over the last twenty years. During the 1980s, the FBI's Uniform Crime Reports (UCR) reported that nearly 2,500 crimes of personal violence and more than 105,000 property crimes were occurring annually on reporting institutions' campuses. In 1990, the UCR reported more than 2,600 violent crimes and approximately 120,000 property crimes occurred on campuses.[9] As cited earlier, recent survey figures now indicate more than three times this number of violent crimes on our nation's campuses.[10] In fact, recent data indicate that in a typical year more than 36,000 violent assaults, 7,500 sexual assaults, dozens of homicides, and some 200,000 thefts will occur on American college campuses.[11] While some may argue that this increase is due, in part, to recently mandated reporting measures, there is little doubt that the occurrence of violent crime on our campuses is on the increase. Incidents of shootings, carjackings, and other crimes of violence simply mirror the alarming number of such felonious crimes being perpetrated in virtually every county and community in America. As in society at large, gun possession and gun violence has now become a common threat to many campuses.

## ADMINISTRATIVE PHILOSOPHY AND POLICIES

College presidents and governing boards are responsible for recognizing the realities of campus crime and they should ensure that institutional policies include statement(s) which reflect their philosophy on the issues of crime and violence or, to some extent, the issue of creating a safe learning environment. It is important that a "zero tolerance" philosophy toward all forms of violence prevail from top administrators to every faculty and staff member on campus. This philosophy should particularly be embraced by student affairs personnel and reflected in the policies and procedures of every student organization. Issues related to crime and security should be afforded a high priority and included in institutional goals and objectives. Both student personnel officials and academic affairs faculty and administrators should develop unit goals, objectives, and programs which support and implement institutional goals on campus safety. This entire issue and phenomenon of campus crime provides higher education officials with an educative opportunity to teach responsible social conduct to include sanctions and consequences associated with criminal behavior.[12] Furthermore, the administrative philosophy on campus crime and security should be translated into direct support to all related campus constituency groups where day-to-day programs and activities deal with real issues and problems.

## IMAGE AND RECRUITMENT

"Welcome, welcome to our campus where you'll find a wide range of curricular offerings, exciting social programs, prestigious faculty, and an outstanding athletic program. Come join us. We're friendly, we give plenty of financial aid, and we're the best college in the state. Our graduates include big time professional athletes, rocket scientists, and brain surgeons." The "welcomes" and enrollment inducements are almost endless from institution to institution—public and private, two-year and four-year, small and large. Student handbooks, curricular catalogues, recruiting brochures, orientation videos, and housing guides depict college students in ultramodern classrooms or walking casually down flower-lined walkways. The "welcomes" are repeated countless times by student affairs personnel during visitation days and orientation sessions. College and university presidents certainly understand the importance of welcoming students and parents to their campuses and extending sincere invitations. They appreciate the significance of promoting their schools' amenities through glossy-paged catalogs and attractive brochures. They support aggressive recruitment efforts to bring the "best and the brightest" to their institutions. However, assiduous college and university leaders will also understand that despite all of their commitments and efforts to portray their institution in positive ways, a crime problem— whether real or perceived—will have a major and debilitating impact on their institution's success.

The image of an institution of higher learning is inextricably linked to that institution's recruitment efforts. Students typically "buy" image. College recruiters visit high school groups, mail marketing advertisements, utilize a variety of media forms, and even plug into telephone marketing techniques all to attract students to their institutions. Through these processes every attempt is made to accentuate all of the amenities and positive aspects of the school. Unfortunately, media reports and word-of-mouth accounts or recent serious crime and violence on the campus will send a chilling message which may diminish those positive portraits painted by college recruiters.

## RETENTION AND RESIDENCE OCCUPANCY: STUDENT VICTIMS

While campus crime impacts an institution's image and recruiting efforts, perhaps equally as important is the effect which crime, violence, and fear of harm can have on students already enrolled. A perceived crime problem may impact an institution's student body in two ways. First, students who believe a serious threat exists may actually withdraw from classes and go home or leave at semester's end. Secondly, students living in campus housing may be influenced by crime or the fear thereof to move to an off-campus location or back home and commute to campus. In either scenario parents may likely play a major role in these decisions.

Many colleges and universities have developed comprehensive retention programs aimed at holding the line on declining enrollment. Student exit surveys and other extensive assessment measures are employed in determining the various factors which influence students to leave school. Often cited are concerns about campus security and more specifically, residence hall security. Informal reports from campus police/security directors indicate that parents usually initiate their children's withdrawal from college due to their own concerns of recently reported crimes of violence (i.e., murder, rape, robbery, etc.). Some students, though not victims themselves gain knowledge of campus violence and crime through rumors, campus newspaper reports, and campus police information.

Residence hall and campus apartment occupancy can be particularly problematic for campus officials. Many institutions already find that enticing students to live on campus is becoming more competitive with off-campus apartment options. In some cases, students may feel safer at these off-campus residences than on campus. The fact is, prior research has shown on-campus residence students to be particularly susceptible to crime.[13] This is not surprising since some features of campus living are actually conducive to antisocial behavior. Typical on-campus residence halls and apartments present unique conditions or factors which may exacerbate incidents of violence between students themselves. A major portion of this population consists of young, single adults who are experiencing freedom from home and parental control for the first time. These "post adolescents or pre-adults," are thrust into a new environment where behavioral controls are minimal and there is no sense of vulnerability. Alcohol is the drug of choice, living arrangements place large numbers of students in close proximity to each other, and diversity is the rule in terms of race, ethnicity, gender, and sexuality. Consequently, when serious crimes do occur, students and especially parents who have expectation of a tranquil, safe campus become alarmed and react by moving off campus or even to another college or university.

## INSTITUTIONAL LIABILITY

Colleges and universities operate in an increasingly litigious climate. Institutions and their officials are subject to a wide range of legal challenges for both their actions or failures to act. No area is more susceptible to plaintiff's allegations than that of campus crime and safety.

Universities across the country are facing increasing numbers of lawsuits against them resulting from incidents of campus violence. The increase in lawsuits by injured students is attributable to a growing recognition that higher education institutions may be held responsible for crime and violence on campus. The American public, especially parents of prospective college students, is shopping more selectively with security as a primary consideration.[14] The public and parents are now more educated about colleges' responsibilities to protect their "customers" and, consequently, parental expectations are high. They are prepared to hold college officials accountable for the safety of their children.

With the abandonment of the *in loco parentis* doctrine, the courts have replaced this "parent-child" relationship theory with three other theories of institutional liability. Courts in every state of the nation recognize the existence of a legal duty to protect others from foreseeable criminal acts, where there is a special relationship between the victim and the protector. This special relationship theory has been defined as "some definite relation between the parties, of such a character that social policy justifies the imposition of a duty to act." A college or university is expected to have an institutional commitment to the welfare and safety of its student. Given this public expectation, most institutions acknowledge their obligation, and subsequently exercise care to protect their students by providing appropriate levels of security. By voluntarily taking this action, unsteadiness of higher education inherently assumes and reinforces the existence of a special relationship with its students.

Another relationship theory is the landowner-business invitee relationship and is recognized as a special relationship for purposes of demonstrating a duty owed in a negligence action. In just such an action against a college or university, the academic institution may be analogized to a landowner owing its students-invitees a duty of care or the duty to use reasonable care to warn and protect invitees from foreseeable dangers.

The third relationship theory often used by the courts is the landlord-tenant relationship. In some states which recognize a higher duty, a landlord must warn a tenant of known or reasonably known dangerous conditions. In the academic context the university-landlord must warn its students-tenants when a reasonably foreseeable danger arises in residence halls or other residence facilities.[15]

Crime on campus is subjecting institutions of higher learning and those who run them to a broad new field of civil liability and monetary damages. Campus decision-makers are at risk unless they take appropriate steps to ensure that students and employees are reasonably protected from crime and violence.[16] In 1994, the Kansas Supreme Court voted 5 to 2 to allow a student to proceed with a civil lawsuit against Kansas State University, ruling that state colleges and universities have a limited, legal duty to protect their students from crime.[17] A Massachusetts Supreme Court reached a similar conclusion in the 1983 case of *Mullins v. Pine Manor College.* The court held that Pine Manor College, a private institution, was responsible for providing reasonable campus security against rape.[18]

Campus crime and violence can result in serious liability to the institution. The very nature and projected image of a college community are subjected to disruption, embarrassment, and negative publicity when lawsuits are filed. Additionally, legal fees and court imposed awards can be costly to institutions already in the throws of retrenchment efforts. Moreover, lawsuits and the attendant publicity may discourage prospective students and parents from considering a particular college or university. The confidence in the campus administration and security measures can be severely damaged. Unfortunately, some lawsuits may not be avoided.[19] It is incumbent on university officials to understand the havoc that can be caused and the long-term impacts of campus crime. Strategies and programs to reduce these impacts are essential to creating a safe campus.

## UNIVERSITY-COMMUNITY ISSUES

Issues often associated with crime, student conduct, and violence that are frequently not recognized as a college or university problem are those associated with town-gown or college and local community relations. Both universities and their local communities impact each other in a variety of ways. In some respects, this might be referred to as a "double-edged" issue in which university students have significant impacts on the local community and the community on the college students. Some institutions' student conduct policies hold students accountable for their off-campus behavior. While other colleges and universities do not consider off-campus behavior an institutional matter, local community officials and residents often expect some institutional control and/or intervention. Provisions in the federal Crime Awareness and Campus Security Act of 1990 require colleges to collect and disclose criminal incidents and arrests at off-campus locations involving student organizations recognized by the institution. Off-campus college-recognized fraternities represents an example of university presence within the community.

The other "edge" of the issue is the responsibility of local officials in "policing" sometimes thousands of college students living near campus but in the local community's jurisdiction. Student conduct and criminal incidents by and against students becomes a community problem for which some university officials and parents expect solutions. While this discussion is aimed primarily at the impact of crime and violence on this issue, there is a myriad of other factors which must be considered in order to gain a proper perspective.

There are some basic assumptions about the university-community environment which should be considered. While not all of these assumptions are applicable to all colleges and universities, they do represent some common characteristics found where institutions of higher education coexist with their local communities. They include:

1. There is a striking difference in nearby neighborhoods when the university is in session and when the students are gone home for the holidays.
2. In most university communities, some students will dwell in off-campus housing.
3. Students' behavior and values will be different from that of the local community members.
4. Students' social activities will frequently create loud noise.
5. Most students drive at least one automobile, consequently resulting in parking and traffic problems on city streets.
6. Local residents living near student houses, apartments, and fraternity residences do not often share the students' taste in music, moral values, bedtime hours, or friends.
7. The students who live in a particular apartment one year may not be there the next, but will be replaced by other students unfamiliar with any previous agreements or regulations.
8. The leadership of fraternities and sororities will usually change from year to year.

9. Off-campus dwellings occupied by college students, particularly older houses, are often allowed to deteriorate by proprietors.
10. The university campus can be detrimentally affected by criminal activity perpetrated by local residents, particularly if the campus is located near a crime-ridden area.
11. The racial and cultural backgrounds of the students will sometimes differ substantially from that of local residents.
12. The academic level, political views, and socioeconomic status of university faculty and administrators usually conflicts with that of many community residents.[20]

As mentioned above, fraternities provide a relatively common case scenario in which crime and student misconduct have serious ramifications on university-community relations. It also represents the jurisdictional/responsibility issue which frequently creates tensions between university officials and local officials and residents. The following is an actual paid advertisement placed in the local newspaper of a town-gown community. The name of the city is changed to protect its identity.

## Concerned Citizens

As citizens of Collegetown, we are a few of many who are fed up with the inconsiderate behavior of the fraternities located throughout our city.

As Fraternity Students' behavior has become a major problem to our city. The police department is required to continually answer calls from the citizens to quiet the noise and bring some form of order to the students' preposterous behavior. They have no regard and openly defy the ordinance on noise and cutoff time for their many social activities.

On September 6, 1988, Pi Sigma Chi Fraternity had a live band with an "estimated crowd of 1,300" (fraternity estimate) in attendance. The party was held outside with speakers and amplifiers on porches, lawns, etc. The volume was turned so high that it actually vibrated the floors and windows of homes for several blocks.

The streets and lawns were littered with empty beer cans and paper cups. Cars were parked on private property blocking drives, preventing people from entering their own drives. Tow trucks were called to tow many away. The main street had cars parked on both sides creating a very hazardous condition for motorists in the area.

After the police went up and talked to them and left, the students yelled over the speakers, "Neighbors, is this loud enough for you?" increasing their yelling and blasting music so loud that it shook our homes. No one could hear his television or phone calls, and other students could not study.

The many elderly and working people, including other university students living in the area, had no rest until 1:30 A.M. when the party was moved inside the fraternity house. The fraternity students continued yelling and carrying on until 3:00 A.M. disturbing residents closer by.

This behavior is not just one or two fraternities, nor is it one-time occurrence. It is a continual one throughout the year.

Although we realize social functions are important to all students, no group should be allowed to show such disregard to the rights of others.

We as citizens feel it is time for the university to assume responsibility of the social fraternities with university and city working together to provide a Fraternity Row and a place for their social functions out of residential areas back on campus under the supervision of the Dean of Students.

Enough is enough. We can assure you that when these affairs are taking place that no one in charge of Student Affairs can be reached. We tried for five hours to reach them. We did reach a person who was previously associated with Student Affairs. Although all of our windows and doors were closed, he could plainly hear over the phone the lambasting we were forced to endure. He assured us he would inform those in charge.

Yes, we want a good university. Higher education is vital. We have always been proud to have the university as part of our city. This type of action is not a part of higher education. It is in our opinion degrading to the university as well as our city.[21]

Off-campus crime, of the serious nature, is increasing throughout the nation. Whether students are victims or perpetrators, its impact on the college or university and its image is important. In fact, as the campus crime issue continues to gain national attention and campus safety becomes a major consideration for college selection, college officials are pressed to deal with the issue. One recent publication, *Crime at College: The Student Guide to Personal Safety,* ranks America's most dangerous college towns along with the on-campus crime rate.[22] No doubt such publications are in response to increasingly well publicized off-campus incidents of violence to include murder. One report published in the December 7, 1994 issue of the *Chronicle of Higher Education* cited eleven incidents in which students were killed in the fall semester of 1994 at off-campus locations near universities.[23] These incidents, mostly shootings, occurred in university communities all over the country to include Tallahassee, Florida; Atlanta, Georgia; Binghamton, New York; Pine Bluff, Arkansas; and College Station, Texas.[24] Some research indicates that on average, a college campus is safer than the city that houses it. Overall, colleges have about one-fifth the level of violent crime as their cities. Similarly, they have about two-thirds the level of property crime.[25]

Crime, violence, and student conduct are university-community issues which impact higher education institutions and their officials. These issues require effective strategies, innovative solutions, and collaborative efforts to reduce the risks and the impacts.

## SUMMARY

The issues and impacts of crime and violence on and off campus should receive the attention of college officials like never before. There are clear indications that as society's ills spills onto our nation's campuses, not only institutional images will suffer, but the quality of life of the campus community will be diminished. Long known for an atmosphere conducive to scholarly pursuits and personal and social growth, the campus should remain relatively unincumbered by threats of violence. For nearly three decades the phenomenon of campus crime has become just another characteristic of the campus environment. College and university administrators have often not understood the issues or recognized the impacts of this injustice to our academic institutions. High on the agenda of every college president for the next century should be to create a safe campus.

## ENDNOTES

1. Jean Evangelauf, "A New Carnegie Classification," *The Chronicle of Higher Education*, Vol. XL, No. 31, April 6, 1994, p. A17.
2. Douglas Lederman, "Colleges Report 7,500 Violent Crimes On Their Campuses in First Annual Statements Required Under Federal Law," *The Chronicle of Higher Education*, Vol. XXXIX, No. 20, January 20, 1993, p. A43.
3. Douglas Lederman, "Colleges Report 7,500 Violent Crimes On Their Campuses in First Annual Statements Required Under Federal Law," *The Chronicle of Higher Education*, Vol. XXXIX No. 20, January 20, 1993, p. A32.
4. John J. Sloan, III and Bonnie S. Fisher, "Providing More Than A Glimpse of the Extent of Crime On Campuses," *The Chronicle of Higher Education*, Vol. XL, No. 26, March 2, 1994, p. B3.
5. Susan B. Morris, "The Influences of Campus Characteristics On College Crime Rates," Presented at the Association of Institutional Research, Chicago, Illinois, May 18, 1993.
6. Crime Awareness and Campus Security Act of 1990, Public Law 101–542, November 8, 1990, 104 Stat. 2385.
7. Towson State University, Center for the Study and Prevention of Campus Violence (1986, 1987, 1988). *National Campus Violence Survey 1986, 1987, 1988 Data Tables.* Towson, MD: Towson State University.

8. Uniform Crime Reports for 1993, U.S. Department of Justice (U.S. Government Printing Office, Washington, D.C., 1993), pp. 4–12.
9. Susan B. Morris, p. 1.
10. Douglas Lederman, p. A32.
11. Michael Clay Smith and Margaret D. Smith, *Wide Awake: A Guide to Safe Campus Living in the 90's,* (Princeton, New Jersey: Peterson's Guides, 1990), p. 1.
12. Michael Clay Smith, *Crime and Campus Police: A Handbook for Police Officers and Administrators,* (Asheville, North Carolina: College Administration Publications, Inc., 1989) p. 6.
13. J.A. Fox and D.A. Hellman, "Location and Other Correlates to Campus Crime," *Journal of Criminal Justice,* 13, 1988, pp. 429–444.
14. Jeffrey A. Newman, Esq., "Crime On the College Campus and Legal Liability Issues," *Campus Law Enforcement Journal,* Vol. 23, No. 6, Nov./Dec., 1993, p. 7.
15. Philip Burling, *Crime On Campus: Analyzing and Managing the Increasing Risk of Institutional Liability,* National Association of College and University Attorneys Publication, 1990, p. 4.
16. Michael Clay Smith, *Coping With Crime On Campus,* (New York: Macmillan Publishing Company, 1988), p. 81.
17. *Campus Security Report,* (Port Washington, New York: Rusting Publications), Vol. 6, No. 1, January 1994, p. 24.
18. Smith, p. 82.
19. John W. Powell, M.S. Pander, and R.C. Nielsen, *Campus Security and Law Enforcement,* (Boston: Butterworth-Heinemann, 1994), p. 247.
20. David Nichols, *University-Community Relations: Living Together Effectively,* (Springfield, Illinois: Charles C Thomas Publisher, 1990), p. 91.
21. Ibid, pp. 92 & 93.
22. Curtis Ostrander and Joseph Schwartz, *Crime at College: The Student Guide to Personal Safety,* (Ithaca, New York: New Strategist Publications, 1994).
23. Douglas Lederman, "A Tragic Toll: At Least 11 Students Have Been Killed This Fall In Off-Campus Locations," *The Chronicle of Higher Education,* Vol. XLT, No. 15, December 7, 1994, p. A35.
24. Ibid, p. A35.
25. Consortium for Higher Education Research, School of Criminal Justice, Hindelang Criminal Justice Research Center, The Nelson A. Rockefeller College of Public Affairs and Policy, University of Albany, Albany, New York, 1994.

# Chapter 3

# THREATS TO A SAFE CAMPUS

## INTRODUCTION

Today's college campus, as in centuries past, is susceptible to the influences of society. It is clear that America's alarming rise in violent crime has not spared our sanctuaries of academe. Along with a few other institutions in our communities once considered relatively safe places such as elementary schools, the post office, and home, colleges and universities have been intruded by unconscionable and random acts of violence. This is not to say that our campuses are ravaged by marauding gangs of killers and rapists. It is to say, however, that they are no longer immune from all of the same threats which plague our schools and communities. Virtually every type of crime that occurs in the city, from murder to rape to riots, has also taken place on campuses across the nation. In order for college officials to develop effective strategies toward a safe campus, they must be cognizant of threats which pose substantial risks to their campuses.

## GUNS ON CAMPUS

In February, 1994, the Association of Student Judicial Affairs unanimously adopted a resolution urging colleges and universities to support through rules and laws to keep guns off campuses.[1] In a 1995 survey of Alabama's campus police/security directors 75 percent reported firearms possession incidents on their campuses within the past three years. Ninety-five percent of respondents said they believe their campuses are at risk to gun violence.[2] Reports of gun violence on campuses across the nation are increasing. In a survey conducted by the *Chronicle of Higher Education* in 1994, campus officials reported a 16 percent increase in the number of weapons violations arrests.[3] Campus police officers are reporting with greater frequency their exposure to weapons possessions. One officer patrolling on a university campus of 7,600 reported his discovery of guns in 4 out of 6 vehicle stops in one week!

In December 1994 on the campus of Jacksonville State University, in Alabama, two students were robbed of their car and one of them shot in the buttocks as he fled. The two masked gunmen drove off in the car and were never captured.

In December 1993, a student at Simon's Rock College, near Great Barrington, Massachusetts fatally shot a professor and fellow student and wounded three other students and a security officer.[4]

In November, 1993 police in Ohio arrested a former Kent State University student and another man in connection with a suspected drug-related shooting incident at the university.

These incidents represent many more similar occurrences of gun-related violence sweeping college and university campuses. Such incidents are reported at small colleges, two-year postsecondary schools, rural campuses, and large urban universities. The proliferation of guns and their availability and usage has had a tremendous influence on both the frequency and seriousness of campus crime. Three decades ago a dispute between college students usually resulted in fisticuffs and a bloody nose. Today, it is more likely to end in a deadly shooting.

It is not surprising that guns and gun-related violence are becoming problematic and commonplace on many campuses. Nonfatal crimes committed with a gun reached a record level in 1992, says the U.S. Justice Department's Bureau of Justice Statistics. The Bureau reported 917,000 such crimes, nearly 50 percent more than the average for the previous five years. According to the U.S. Department of Justice, Federal Bureau of Investigation's 1993 Uniform Crime Report, firearms were the weapons used in 7 out of 10 murders in 1993. Of those murders by weapons, 57 percent were by handguns. Nationwide, firearms were used in over 25 percent of aggravated assaults in 1993. This national phenomenon has become an epidemic, spreading to every town, city, and borough of the country.

This violence epidemic is also taking its toll on our elementary and secondary schools. According to statistics from the Harvard School of Public Health and Centers for Disease Control, about 135,000 guns are brought into elementary and secondary schools every day. The survey also reveals that firearms are the leading cause of death for African American males aged 15–24. They are the second leading cause of death for all American teens. About 10 percent of all youth surveyed (aged 10–19) say that they have fired a gun at someone or have been shot at.[5]

While experts argue as to the extent, many of these youngsters who develop a tolerance to guns and violence in high school virtually bring their guns and dispositions to campus along with their enrollment packets. Guns are showing up in residence halls, in automobiles, at concerts, at athletic events, at parties, and even in classrooms. They are found in coat pockets, bookbags, trousers, and purses. Incidents in which guns are discovered on campus may represent only the tip of the iceberg of the actual number of guns possessed on campus. University policies banning firearms possession have had little deterrent effect since virtually all institutions have such prohibitions. The increased use of metal detectors at special events only underscores the problem. Some colleges located near larger cities experience serious gun-related incidents which are gang-related or perpetrated by nonstudents on student victims. Drive-by shootings on campus are becoming more common. However, students themselves are often the culprits. As discussed in the previous chapter, off-campus incidents near the campus often involve guns and violence to include murder. These off-campus incidents are not reserved for big city locations. Two examples illustrate this. Bethune-Cookman College in Daytona Beach, Florida, an institution of about 2,300 students was the site of such a gun-related killing. In 1993, two students and a friend were murdered near the campus there.[6] On November 12, 1992, Dr. Douglas Kingdon, associate professor of education at the University of Tennessee at Chattanooga was shot twice in the head and once in the arm in a robbery/carjacking attempt one block off campus.[7]

Guns on campus represent a serious threat to a safe campus. Unfortunately, some college administrative officials are reluctant to admit that their campus is at risk. They cite few or no reported gun-related incidents and declare that because their policy prohibits guns that they have no real threat. Other higher education officials admit some risk exists but are not realistic in terms of the current vulnerability as evidenced by a clear absence of meaningful programming and security measures.

## VIOLENCE, ASSAULTS, AND HARASSMENT

Violence in this country has become an important issue to the American public from the local level to the national forum. Whether random violence is a threat to most Americans or whether their perceptions have created exaggerated fears, the reality is that people are afraid in the cities, on the highways, and at home. This widespread concern over crime and violence culminated in the passage of the Violent Crime Control and Law Enforcement Act of 1994, also known as the "Crime Bill." This Act was signed into law by President Bill Clinton on September 12, 1994. It represents a multi-billion dollar appropriated effort to get crime under control and provide more police officers on the streets.

Campus violence, assaults, and harassment are on the rise parallel to the increase in American society. While some reports of campus violence include off-campus incidents, they are usually related to the college's presence and/or the presence of college students. In the September 28, 1992 edition of *Atlanta Journal Constitution,* an extensive story exposed the issue of campus violence at southeast colleges and universities. The author described beatings, armed robberies, mob violence, and slayings of students on or near college campuses. Included in this report were the following incidents which all occurred in September:

> *University of North Carolina,* Chapel Hill Sept. 4: Two attempted sexual assaults on campus walkways. Sept. 12: Female students attacked and sprayed with her own mace on campus walkway.
>
> *University of Virginia,* Charlottesville Sept. 3 and Sept. 4: Attempted rape of student by nonstudent at fraternity party, attack on students in dormitory area and beating of student by nonstudent in parking lot.
>
> *University of Miami,* Coral Gables Sept. 9: Two male students robbed at gunpoint near library.
>
> *Florida State University,* Tallahassee Sept. 11: Two male students beaten by a group of nonstudents.
>
> *Florida A & M University,* Tallahassee Sept. 7: White male brutally beaten by a mob of black students angry at police for alleged brutality.
>
> *University of South Carolina,* Columbia Sept. 10: Student assaulted and robbed by man in campus parking lot.[8]

The violence is not limited to colleges in the Southeast. A Missouri court convicted a fraternity president at Southeast Missouri State University in connection with the death of a student pledge in February, 1994.[9] In May, 1994, a former spokesman for the Nation of Islam was shot while delivering a speech during a campus appearance at the University of California-Riverside.[10] In March, 1994, four students were abducted from a campus parking lot of Rice University in Houston, Texas.[11]

Violence also takes on many forms other than gun-related violence. It includes, but is not limited to, other weapons-related assaults, physical assaults, threats of violent acts, and rape and sexual assaults. For the purpose of this discussion violence will refer to acts or threats of personal injury with the exception of rape and sexual assault. While the proliferation of guns and gun violence are societal problems and certainly threaten a safe campus, the overwhelming incidents of violence on college campuses are of a much less serious nature. A common form of campus violence is the simple assault and battery, usually a misdemeanor. These incidents occur most often in residence halls and at social and athletic events, especially where drugs and alcohol are consumed. In many cases these incidents are never reported, yet, can create a hostile environment for students.

A less frequent but more serious type of violence is aggravated assault. Such incidents do occur on most college campuses throughout the country but with less frequency than simple assaults. The U.S. Department of Justice Federal Bureau of Investigation's Uniform Crime Report defines aggravated assault as "an unlawful attack by one person upon another for the purpose of inflicting severe or aggravated bodily injury." This type of assault is usually accompanied by the use of a weapon or by means likely to produce death or great bodily harm. Attempts are included. Again, most aggravated assaults occur in and around residence halls and at social events. Alcohol and other drugs are common factors in both simple assaults and aggravated assaults. A study conducted in 1987 by Towson State University found that alcohol was believed to be a frequent and common factor in all physical assaults. Most responding institutions reported that greater than 50 percent of all types of violence was alcohol-related.[12] Aggravated assaults create serious threats to the student body as well as faculty and staff. Whereas, simple assaults seldom get media attention, aggravated assaults can become public relations issues for college administrators.

Harassment comes in many forms. Sexual harassment has received national attention as a result of the Clarence Thomas Hearings in which Anita Hill accused the U.S. Supreme Court nominee of sexual harassment while she was his subordinate employee. Usually sexual harassment complaints come from women against men. On the college campus this often involves faculty women in the workplace. In one survey of 30,000 faculty, about 15 percent of women said they had been sexually harassed compared to only 3 percent of men. Female students may also be the recipients of sexual harassment by faculty and staff members. This same study revealed that about 2 million female college students face sexual harassment, indicating a much larger problem than facing faculty members.[13] One such case was reported at Swarthmore College in Pennsylvania. A female student there accused a male faculty member of making harassing telephone calls to her, lurking outside her classes, entering her residence hall room without permission, and making at least one menacing gesture toward her.[14] This is not a particularly uncommon example of campus sexual harassment. Sexual harassment in any form or in any type of relationship is a threat to a safe campus and the sense of dignity and peace expected by the campus community.

In addition to harassment of women on campus, other groups are often targeted for intimidation and harassment. Among these are racial/ethnic minorities, homosexuals, and some religious groups. The number of minority and international students studying at U.S. colleges and universities has continued to increase year after year. Academic institutions across the country have experienced a resurgence of prejudicial insensitivity and related violence. Violence done to members of those groups that have historically been disenfranchised—such as gays and racial and ethnic minorities—continues to go unreported. Vandalism seems to occur with greater frequency than in the past.[15] Intolerance of racial and ethnic difference, religious preference, and sexual orientation has resulted in incidents of assaults, cross burning, vandalism, offensive posters or flyers, intimidating telephone calls, and threatening letters.

In a study conducted to examine victimization in residence halls, survey results revealed that the 5,526 "reported" incidents represented perhaps only 28 percent of the 20,000 incidents believed to have taken place. These incidents were categorized into "violence," "vandalism," and "verbal harassment." The groups identified as victim groups were women, racial/ethnic minorities, gay/lesbian, Jewish, and resident assistants. This study summarized:

> However, it should be clearly stated that although many of the incidents resulting in racial violence began at the verbal level, most verbal abuse and vandalism perpetrated against minority students did not result in violence. Rather, minority students, along with gay/lesbian students and Jewish students, bear the burden of being continuously victimized by offensive, taunting, tormenting behaviors on the part of other students. Although some may be tempted to define incidents of vandalism and verbal harassment as "minor," it is emphasized that words like "nigger" and symbols like swastikas cause pain and suffering to many students who perceive their residence hall and campus environment not only as cold, unwelcoming, and insensitive, but downright hos-

tile and intimidating. Such environments are clearly far from the ideal ones that would be conducive to the learning, growth, and development of our students.[16]

It should be pointed out that minority groups are not the only recipients of harassment. In some incidents white students have been victimized by minority students and male students have been harassed by female students. White students who attend predominately black institutions may experience many of the same biases which African-American students face on some predominately white campus. For example, white and Hispanic students complained to the administration at Evergreen State College in Tacoma, Washington that discrimination against them at this predominately black institution occurred on more than one occasion.[17]

Higher education institutions are scholarly environments which celebrate diversity. Policies and programs aimed at transitioning students of different cultures, races, and backgrounds abound on most campuses. Many institutions have created positions and units devoted to minority recruitment, activities, academic success, and special needs. Despite these efforts, college and university officials find that racial tensions and harassment among the many racial tensions and harassment among the many diverse student groups continue to be realities. The climate created by these behaviors is not conducive to academic and social freedom required for a safe campus. Further, these incidents present problems for campus officials in their efforts to create safe campus environments.

## HAZING

Hazing may be in the form of harassment or assault to include serious physical harm. Hazing on college campuses in this country has resulted in dozens of deaths and countless victims of hazing have suffered injuries or long-term emotional and psychological consequences. Hazing activities which often begin as fun and games can result in tragedy. Most colleges and universities have hazing prohibition policies. More than 23 states have enacted statutes making hazing illegal.[18] The Code of Alabama defines hazing as:

   (1) Any willful action taken or situation created, whether on or off any school, college, university, or other educational premises, which recklessly or intentionally endangers the mental or physical health of any student, or

   (2) Any willful act on or off any school college, university, or other educational

premises by any person alone or acting with others in striking, beating, bruising, or maiming; or seriously offering, threatening, or attempting to strike, beat, bruise, or maim, or to do or seriously offer, threaten, or attempt to do physical violence to any student of any such institution or any assault upon any such students made for the purpose of committing any of the acts, or producing any of the results to do such student as defined in this section.[19]

Incidents of hazing threaten a safe campus in several ways. The practice of hazing creates an intimidating climate where such behavior often becomes socially sanctioned by some groups of students. Students often voluntarily endure a variety of hazing activities from marching under duress to being physically assaulted. Consequently, they may suffer physical and emotional scars. Hazing can also carry with it criminal liability. While hazing is usually a misdemeanor, the acts involved may constitute a felony. Criminal liability for hazing extends beyond the persons who actually commit the hazing act. Under principles of accomplice liability, persons may be liable for the crimes of another if they assist or encourage the crime. Furthermore, there may be institutional liability for the college or university which recognized the fraternity, sorority, or other group. Whether a "special relationship" is a basis for suit or negligence, institutional officials should understand the seriousness of hazing and its threat to a safe campus.

While hazing is usually associated with campus Greek organizations, it is not limited to these groups. For example, a former drummer for the Michigan State University band who said he was hazed by band members, won a $100,000 judgement against the university and a former percussion director. The jury found that Michigan State University had not done enough to protect the victim.[20]

## RAPE AND OTHER SEX OFFENSES

Rape has become a serious and, sometimes, confusing issue for college and university officials. Rape is the simple, most examined and discussed campus crime among campus police, student affairs personnel, student health officials, and top administrators. The topic has received wide attention by the national media, at conferences, in professional publications, and by scholarly researchers. News stories and magazines often sensationalize the issue of campus rape insinuating that coeds are ravaged by rapists who lurk around corners and in bushes. Some well-intentioned victims of tragic rape incidents go on T.V. talk shows and attempt to indict college officials for their apathy. Campus police and deans of students are often portrayed as insensitive and deceptive and who go to great lengths to cover up the truth about campus rape. Consequently, perceptions about campus rape may be significantly inaccurate. Research, by and large, indicates that stranger rape on campus is far less frequent than other crimes such as date or acquaintance rapes, physical assaults, vandalism, and theft. Yet, some do occur and often in and around residence halls and parking lots. Some rapes on college students actually occur just off campus in apartments or cars but are considered campus related incidents. Stranger rapes are reported at higher rates than rapes committed by acquaintances. These incidents usually create more widespread panic and fear throughout the campus community than do date rapes.

Acquaintance rape, also known as date rape, is the most frequently committed type of rape and the least reported. In a study conducted at Stanford University, findings revealed that one-third of female graduate students and over one-fourth of female undergraduate students indicate that they have been coerced into sex. The women surveyed say that about 55 percent of those assaults took place while they attended Stanford. About 98 percent of them reported that the person who coerced them was an acquaintance.[21]

In a more comprehensive study of rape on 32 colleges and universities, Dr. Mary Koss, a clinical psychologist and her staff interviewed some 3,000 men and about 3,200 women. Survey highlights include:

- One in five students had been raped by men they knew
- One in eight women were victims of rape or attempted rape in the year prior to the study
- 84 percent knew their attacker and 57 percent of the incidents happened on dates
- Only five percent reported the rapes to police
- In acquaintance rape incidents, about 75 percent of the males and 55 percent of the women had been drinking or taking drugs just before the attack
- Most rapes were off campus and occurred in either the person's home or car.[22]

Other sex offenses also pose a threat to a safe campus. These include such incidents as sodomy, sexual misconduct, indecent exposure, and sexual abuse. Voyeurism is also a menace on some campuses and sometimes creates widespread panic among coeds. Obscene telephone calls may also fit this category since sexually explicit language serves to offend the receiver. These offenses, though usually less serious than rape, may be more commonplace on a college campus than in some communities. This may be due, in part, to the higher concentration of young, single females within residence halls and apartments. Often "locals" loiter on and around campus hoping to prey on unsuspecting college women. This problem is further exacerbated by the absence of caution exercised by most college students who do not recognize their vulnerability.

Sex offenses and sexual aggression can have a devastating impact on victims as well as institutions of higher education. More sex-related cases are emerging and most have potential for criminal prosecution. Also, civil legal actions seeking monetary judgments are increasingly resulting from sex-related offenses on campus. It behooves campus administrators to recognize that the college campus community is an environment in which sex offenses have long been known to flourish and understand the significant threat posed to students. Failure to respond to foreseeable threats may result in higher rates of victimization and negligence complaints against the institution. The knowledge that date rape is underreported, as well as a crime about which victims may be confused, supports an institutional obligation to address the issue and other sex-related offenses and provide victim assistance and preventive educational programs.[23]

## ALCOHOL AND DRUGS

The use of alcohol and drugs in the last 25 years has become a major societal problem. The use of these substances has been attributed to more than half of all fatal traffic accidents, most domestic disputes involving violence, and a large number of homicides. They often prove to be a significant factor in gang violence and other street crimes. Many campus law enforcement officials believe that alcohol and drug abuse is the number one problem which threatens campus safety and security today. While illegal drug possession and use on college campuses remain a concern for university administrators, alcohol has become the primary substance abuse issue on most campuses. Campus police and security directors agree that alcohol is the significant factor in crimes committed on campus. This does not mean that the use of other drugs has, in fact, declined and is no longer problematic to the academic environment.[24]

Alcohol consumption has long been a part of the collegiate experience. An independent commission studying substance abuse on American campuses found that although excessive drinking among the general population has decreased, it continues to increase among college students. The Commission on Substance Abuse at Colleges and Universities, established by the Center on Addiction and Substance Abuse (ASA) at Columbia University, found evidence that excessive drinking puts students at risk for AIDS, rape, violence, and unplanned pregnancies. One in three college students—most of them underage—now drink primarily to get drunk, and nearly one-half has engaged in binge drinking (consuming at one sitting five or more cans of beer, five or more glasses of wine or five or more hard liquor drinks of 1 to 1.5 ounces each).[25]

In a 1989 survey entitled "Linking the Use of Drugs/Alcohol and Student Crime," conducted by the Campus Violence Prevention Center at Towson State University the following findings were reported:

1. Student perpetrators of crime tend to be more frequent drug and alcohol users than either their victims or students who have not been associated with any sort of crime. Alcohol and drug use further appear to be a victimization risk factor since student victims of crime tend to be more frequent than do students who have not been associated with crimes of any sort since enrolling in college.
2. Students who commit multiple offenses tended to use drugs and alcohol even more frequently than students who had committed a single crime. Similarly, students who had been victimized more than once tended to report more frequent overall drug and alcohol use than students who had been victimized only once.
3. Based on a construction of reliable victim and perpetrator profiles, it was determined that victims of student crime tended to:
   a. be more frequent illicit drug users
   b. use more alcohol
   c. be slightly older
   d. be a fraternity/sorority member
   e. own a car, have a job, live off campus, and
   f. be more likely to smoke[26]
   Perpetrators tended to be:
   a. even more frequent drug, alcohol, and cigarette users
   b. male
   c. athletes or fraternity/sorority members, and
   d. have slightly lower grade point averages

The use of illegal drugs also continues to plague colleges and universities. In a study surveying 56,361 students on 78 institutions, researchers at Southern Illinois University found that 21 percent of students reported using marijuana on a less-than-weekly basis and 6 percent used marijuana on a weekly or more frequent basis. Students participating in the study reported cocaine use in the last year.[27]

Alcohol and drugs are prevalent on many college campuses. They become key factors in student misconduct and a wide variety of criminal behavior. This seems most preponderant during social events, in residence halls, and at athletic events. Alcohol and fraternity parties are infamous for gang rapes, binge drinking, hazing, fights, and disruption. As presented above, alcohol and drugs are found to be factors in date rape, assaults, and other violent behavior. Alcohol abuse and illegal drug use also take their toll in psychological and emotional impacts on college students as they struggle to achieve in their rigorous academic pursuits. Alcohol abuse and illegal drug use tends to create a hostile environment for other students and will likely diminish the quality of student life on campus. And finally, alcohol-related behavior can result in serious liability for college officials. One research survey found that ten percent of reporting institutions said they had been sued in alcohol-related incidents.[28]

Congress became so concerned about alcohol and drugs at higher education institutions that the Drug-Free Schools and Communities Act of 1989 included provisions for required policies and programs at all colleges and universities. Yet, regardless of legislative mandates and funding of programs, college students will continue to be a concentrated population of drinkers. College administrators must be vigilant to monitor the changing attitudes and behaviors of their communities and respond with effective measures pertaining to alcohol and illegal drugs. Failure to do so could have serious and costly ramifications for the institution.[29]

## OUTSIDE INTRUDERS

Another threat to a safe campus is that of outside intruders or nonstudents. While statistics indicate that most campus crime is perpetrated by students on other students, significant threats also come from nonstudents. In fact, some campuses experience more nonstudent violent crimes than student-perpetrated incidents. Virtually, every campus is susceptible to these threats. In fact, some smaller institutions such as Birmingham-Southern College in Birmingham, Alabama have perimeter fences aimed at restricted access to campus property by uninvited, and unwanted persons. College and university officials as well as parents of college students tend to perceive outsiders as the greatest threat to students. While this is arguable, the focus of most security measures (i.e., campus police, access control, and procedures) is directed toward outside intruders.

This is true of small private colleges, two-year postsecondary institutions, and large urban campuses. Some campuses have "no trespassing" signs posted at entrances and others display specific directions for visitors entering the campus. Security access gates are used by a few colleges and actually require identification from those entering the campus property.

In the 1987 Towson State University study discussed earlier, student affairs officers, campus police officials, and residence directors from 764 institutions believe that nearly 30 percent of campus assaults were perpetrated by nonstudents.[30] At Oklahoma City University, campus police officials reported 164 criminal trespassing arrests of nonstudents in a five year period.[31] Public safety officials at Jacksonville State University in Alabama, estimate that 18 percent of all on-campus arrests are nonstudents. In fact, all of the three shootings resulting in injuries or death in the past decade were committed by nonstudents.

Local community-based gangs have been the root of some on-campus crime problems across the nation. Most campuses remain in an open-access mode in terms of access by vehicle. City streets typically run through campuses and/or serve as perimeter streets on several boundaries of the campus. The urban campuses of the University of Arkansas at Little Rock are examples of this. There, thefts have increased as gang members drift onto campuses. The result is an increased rate.[32]

In 1988, a female student at Duke University was brutally raped inside her on-campus residence hall by a nonstudent intruder who was later captured and convicted of rape. Also at Duke, in 1992, a man who had just escaped from jail about sixty miles away took four people hostage at gunpoint. After a long standoff with police, he was shot and critically wounded by a police marksman.[33]

The extent of problems by nonstudent intruders will vary from institution to institution. However, one thing is clear. The serious threat posed by nonstudent intruders is real. Problems caused by these outsiders are significant because college and university officials have little or no control over variables that might affect their conduct. Campus regulations for students, faculty, and staff are not persuasive authority to intruders.[34] A case in point is the typical campus policy prohibiting guns on campus. Such a policy and its sanctions can be meaningful to student violators. However, nonstudents who come on campus armed with both a firearm and a legal permit create complex problems for campus authorities. Higher education administrators should recognize that nonstudent intruders represent another threat to a safe campus. Effective strategies should be in place to reduce the associated risks.

## DISORDERS AND DISRUPTIONS

There is one general type of crime and/or misconduct which has plagued the college campus since as far back as the early 1800s—disorders and disruptions. As described in chapter one, these incidents were perhaps the most serious of crime during those years. Often they resulted in serious injury, as at the University of Virginia during the 1830s and 1840s. Rioting there reached a crescendo of violence which resulted in the death of a professor and armed constables being brought to campus to restore order.[35] Then, during the tumultuous 1960s, another wave of civil disobedience and riots impacted college campuses from coast to coast. Today, while no single issue on the national agenda seems to be sweeping campuses, disorders, disruptions, and crises continue to crop up, usually unexpectedly. Perhaps more importantly, as we move toward the twenty-first century of an increasing global economy and social and economic woes at home, it is probable that national issues will again ignite on our nation's campuses. Those campus officials who are responsible for creating a safe campus should attempt to recognize circumstances and indicators which forecast potential crises.

Disorder and disruption can include a laundry list of incidents and conduct. While the focus of riots and disruption during the 1960s centered on the Vietnam War civil rights and a general reaction to the "establishment," today's occurrences are more sporadic and unrelated to any national issue. There is no attempt here to present an all-inclusive list but, rather, to offer some poignant discussion on disorders and disruptions as threats to a safe campus environment.

One of the most frequently reported types of large-scale campus disruption is crowd violence and disorder at social events. On April 18, 1989, on the campus of Jacksonville State University, a fraternity step show/dance erupted into fighting between fraternity members and visiting nonstudents. On-site police officers intervened unsuccessfully to stop the initial fighting. Two arrests were made immediately at the risk to officers. Two incidents of police misconduct were eventually verified, resulting in disciplinary action. The fallout of this crisis was tremendous. News media reports magnified every detail of the incident, sometimes confusing facts with rumors. Such terms as "riot," "fracas," and "racial tensions" preempted the official findings. In essence, the entire episode was a public relations nightmare.

Campus public safety officials at colleges and universities across the country report brawls and fighting among students at fraternity houses, at open parties, athletic events, and at rock concerts held on campus. In most instances these disruptions are spontaneous and happen without warning. Such an incident can be precipitated from a student accidentally bumping into another or over a disagreement about any number of insignificant issues. Whatever the reasons, the dynamics of a large crowd at close quarters coupled with alcohol and drug use provide the ingredients for an explosive incident with ramifications far beyond the initial dispute.

Unfortunately, racial and cultural prejudice and tensions continue to exist on many college campuses despite extensive efforts of administrators to encourage diversity and harmony. Racial issues often evolve into disputes and disputes erupt into violence. In April, 1992, racial tensions between black and white students at Olivet College in Michigan reached a climax with a full-scale brawl in a residence hall lobby involving seventy students. Two students, one black and one white, were injured and briefly hospitalized. Fifty-three black students left campus and returned home following the incident citing threats of violence from townspeople and white students. Immediately after the brawl, eight Pinkerton security guards were called to the campus to patrol, escort students to campus, and monitor residence facilities.[36]

In January, 1995, hundreds of Rutgers University black and Latino students disrupted a televised men's basketball game to protest alleged racial remarks made earlier by the school's president. They also marched to the president's office door in an effort to force him to resign.[37]

Student demonstrations and building takeovers are one of the most stressful events which may occur on a university campus. Whether scheduled or unscheduled, these disruptions to the campus atmosphere can result in uncontrolled behavior, injuries, and a major crisis. Recent campus protests involve gay and lesbian groups, groups supporting and opposing abortion, civil rights activists, environmental groups, animal rights extremists, radical political organizations, and even faculty members protesting contract negotiations. Animal rights extremists, for example, have created widespread disruptions. In 1990, the Association of American Medical Colleges conducted a survey which revealed that within the last five years 76 schools reported damages or other losses totaling in excess of $2.2 million as a result of break-ins, demonstrations, vandalism, and other disruptive incidents.[38] Disorders and disruptions which often accompany these protests seriously threaten the safe campus community.

## PROPERTY CRIMES

In the first year of required reporting under the Right To Know and Campus Security Act, colleges and universities' crime statistics revealed that property crimes, such as burglary (32,127) and motor vehicle theft (8,981), vastly outnumbered violent crimes which totaled 7,500. These property crime categories do not include even a greater number of thefts which occur most frequently in and around residence halls. Since the Right To Know and Campus Security Act does not require higher education officials to collect or report statistics for minor property crimes such as vandalism and theft of property, it is difficult to determine the extent of the property crime problem. However, a look at just two institutions' crime statistics is revealing.

In its 1992 Annual Report, the Department of Police and Security at the University of Wisconsin at Madison indicated only twelve reported violent crimes (murder, rape, robbery, and aggravated assault). The reported property crimes totalled 1,241 (burglary, theft, motor vehicle theft, and arson). In its 1994 Annual Report, the University of Alabama's crime statistics revealed 33 reported violent crimes and 732 reported property crimes.

The occurrence of property crimes on campus typically do not raise grave concerns as do crimes of violence. Nevertheless, they pose a threat to a safe campus and must be considered a high priority for campus officials. Faculty, staff and students who become victims of burglary, theft and vandalism feel personally violated. Their possessions often have sentimental value and cannot be replaced. Further, students and employees have a certain expectation that their personal belongings should be secure while on the campus. Consequently, students and employees hold campus police and security officials accountable for their losses, even though crime prevention is a shared responsibility between security staff and all members of the campus community.

Property crimes are, by and large, perpetrated by students on other students. When this occurs in residence halls, the number of suspects acquainted with the victim is great, thus making it difficult to solve the crime. It is somewhat comparable to theft among family at home—everyone could be a suspect. Many students do not recognize their vulnerability to these crimes and do not take common sense precautions to secure their property.

Some burglaries, thefts, and vandalism are committed by outside intruders—nonstudents. The extent of this problem will be determined to some degree by the demographics of the surrounding community, level of access control to the campus, and facility security measures. Burglary of motor vehicles is often committed by intruders. This is particularly problematic for campuses in urban settings. Remote and unlighted parking areas are prime targets for these perpetrators.

Bicycle theft is certainly no stranger to any college campus. It is not unusual for a large urban university to be faced with six to twelve bicycle thefts a week with a yearly loss of $50,000. The estimated losses for Boston area colleges in 1989 was $500,000. Harvard University officials discovered that their bicycle thefts were being committed by local area youths who were systematically ripping them off. Tufts University and the Massachusetts Institute of Technology also experienced dramatic increases in thefts of one thousand dollar mountain bikes.[39]

Vandalism is a frequently occurring property crime on campus. According to a national study conducted by three researchers on campus crime, vandalism tends to be more often associated with some sort of social activity, such as parties, and is more likely to be committed within the dormitory or other group living milieu. Also, perpetrators of vandalism also tend to be high on alcohol at the time of the incident.[40] Vandalism includes the destruction or defacing of property such as buildings, vehicles, equipment, and works of art.

Property crimes should not be ignored by higher education officials when addressing issues of threat and risk to the campus community. High rates of burglary, theft, and vandalism create dissatisfaction and worries among students and employees. The quality of life on campus is significantly diminished along with the confidence of students and parents in the administration of the institution.

A final area of criminal offenses not included in the FBI's Uniform Crime Reports' crime categories is hate crime. These bias-motivated acts are, unfortunately, found on campuses throughout the country. Hate crimes are not separate distinct offenses, but rather traditional crimes motivated by the offender's bias. An offender may, for example, commit an assault because of his/her bias against the victim's religion, race, ethnicity, or sexual orientation. In response to the passage of the Hate Crime Statistics Act of 1990, the U.S. Attorney General designated the

FBI's UCR Program to develop a collection system to receive hate crime data from its 16,000 law enforcement agency participants. During 1993, 7,587 bias-motivated criminal incidents were reported to the FBI. Of these, 62 percent were motivated by racial bias; 17 percent by religious bias; 11 percent by sexual orientation bias; and the remainder by ethnicity/national origin bias. Intimidation was the single most frequently reported hate crime. However, sixteen persons were murdered in hate-motivated incidents. Racial bias motivated the highest number of murders in 1993 with nine such murders reported. Anti-white offenses accounted for 6 of the 9 homicides. Eighty colleges and universities reported one or more incidents of hate crimes in 1993. One university alone reported 15 race-motivated hate crimes. This is an alarming trend.[41]

## SUMMARY

There are many threats to a safe campus. It is important that college chief executive officers and their key administrators recognize the nature and scope of these threats as they relate to the unique campus environment. Some threats are foreseeable and appropriate preventive measures are easy to develop. On the other hand, some threats may not be readily anticipated and represent greater risks for officials. These unforeseen threats require special leadership and a commitment to ensure that every student, employee, and visitor to the campus is afforded a reasonably safe and secure environment. Most threats can be significantly reduced through the collaborative efforts of all campus officials coupled with a "shared responsibility" philosophy by all campus constituencies. Institutions of higher learning are on the cutting edge of technology, communications, economics, and social reform. Through their mission of research, teaching, and public service, these scholarly institutions must be exemplary as change agents in demonstrating to society that communities can turn the tide of crime and violence and create safe environs for their children.

## ENDNOTES

1. Douglas Lederman, "Weapons On Campus?", *The Chronicle of Higher Education,* Vol. XL, No. 27, March 9, 1994, p. A33.
2. David Nichols, "Guns On Campus Survey," Conducted in January, 1995. Results from 24 responding Campus Police and Security Directors in Alabama.

3. Lederman, p. A34.

4. Christopher Shea, "Simon's Rock College Wrestles With Questions Over Shooting That Left 2 Dead, 4 Wounded," *The Chronicle of Higher Education*, Vol. XXXIX No. 18, January 6, 1993, p. A39.

5. Harvard School of Public Health, Louis Harris Poll as cited in *Education Week*, August 4, 1993; and Centers for Disease Control, "The Battle Over Gun Control," as cited in Black Enterprise Magazine, July 1993. Complied by the Center for Demographic Policy, Washington, D.C.

6. *Campus Security Report*, (Port Washington, New York: Rusting Publications, 1994), Vol. 6, No. 1, January 1994, p. 15.

7. *Campus Security Report*, Vol. 5, No. 2, February, 1993, p. 1.

8. Tinah Saunders, "Rising tide of crime brings fear to South's college campuses," *The Atlanta Journal/The Atlanta Constitution*, September 28, 1992, pp. A1 and A8.

9. *Campus Crime*, (Business Publishers, Inc.: Silver Springs, Maryland, 1994) Vol. 8, No. 8, p. 118.

10. Ibid, Vol. 4, No. 6, p. 58.

11. Ibid, Vol. 4, No. 4, p. 37.

12. Towson State University National Survey of Campus Violence, 1987: Summary Report, Towson, Maryland.

13. Campus Crime, "Report Finds Harassment Affecting Women Faculty—(Silver Springs, Maryland: Business Publishers, Inc., 1994), Vol. 4, No. 5, May 1994, p. 42.

14. "Sexual Harassment At Swarthmore," *Synfax Bulletin*, January 16, 1994, Edited by Gary M. Pavela, Synfax, Inc., Crofton, Maryland, p. 175.

15. Jan M. Sherrill and Dorothy Siegal, *Responding to Violence On Campus*, "New Directions for Student Services No. 47," (San Francisco: Jossey-Bass Publishers: 1989), p. 1.

16. Carolyn J. Palmer, *Violent Crimes and Other Forms of Victimization In Residence Halls*, (Asheville, North Carolina: College Administration Publications, Inc., 1993), pp 48 and 49.

17. Peter Monaghan, "Charges of Bias Against Whites Erupt at Evergreen State Branch," *The Chronicle of Higher Education*, Vol. XLI, No. 24, February 24, 1995 p. A38.

18. Douglas R. Richmond, "The Legal Implications of Fraternity Hazing", *National Association of Student Personnel Administrators Journal*, Vol. 26, No. 4, Summer 1989, page 300.

19. Code of Alabama, Recompiled 1975, Title 16 (16-1-23).

20. *The Chronicle of Higher Education*, "Note Book" Vol. XLI, No. 8, October 19, 1994, p. A55.

21. Alejandro Martinez, "Rape Education Project", Cowell Student Health Center, Stanford University Stanford, California, 1988.

22. Mary Koss, "The Scope of Rape: Incidence and Prevalence of Sexual Aggression and Victimization in a National Sample of Students in Higher Education", *Journal of Consulting and Clinical Psychology*, Vol. 55, No. 2, 1987, pp. 162–170.

23. Spring J. Walton, "Date Rape: New Liability for Colleges and Universities?" *National Association of Student Personnel Administrators Journal,* Vol. 31, No. 3, Spring 1994.

24. *Crime and Transgressions On College/University Campuses,* International Association of Campus Law Enforcement Administrators, Hartford, Connecticut, 1988–89 p. 5.

25. *NASPA FORUM,* "College Student Drinking Continues To Rise," National Association of Student Personnel Administrators, Vol. 14, No. 8, June/July 1994 p. 1.

26. R. Barker Bausell, Carole R. Bausell, and Dorothy G. Siegel, "The Links Among Alcohol, Drugs, and Crime on American College Campuses: A National Follow-up Study" (Business Publishers, Inc., 1990), pp. 3–5.

27. Cheryl A. Presley and Philip W. Meilman, "Alcohol and Drugs on American College Campuses: A Report to College Presidents", Southern Illinois University. A study funded by a grant by the Drug Prevention in Higher Education Program of the Fund for the Improvement of Postsecondary Education (FIPSE), U.S. Department of Education, Washington, D.C., 1992.

28. G.M. Gonzalez, "Alcohol use and level at Knowledge about alcohol among students who visited Daytona Beach, Florida during spring break, 1981. BACCHUS of the U.S. Inc., Gainesville, Florida, University of Florida, 1981.

29. Donald D. Gehing and Cristy P. Geraci, *Alcohol On Campus: A compendium of the law and a guide to campus policy,* (Asheville, North Carolina, College Administration Publications, Inc., 1989, p. 12.

30. Towson State University, 1987.

31. Scott Prough, "Trespassing Arrests as Deterrents," *Campus Law Enforcement Journal,* Vol. 21, No. 4, July/August 1991, p. 31.

32. *Campus Security Report,* Vol. 6, No. 1, January 1994, p. 8.

33. John W. Powell, Michael S. Pander, and Robert C. Nielson, *Campus Security and Law Enforcement,* Second Edition, (Boston, Massachusetts: Butterworth-Heineman, 1994), p. 14.

34. Michael C. Smith, *Coping With Crime On Campus,* (New York: American Council On Education and Macmillan Publishing Company, 1988), p. 19.

35. John S. Brubacker and Willis Rudy, *Higher Education In Transition,* 3rd Ed. (New York: Harper & Row, 1976), p. 53.

36. *Campus Security Report,* Vol. 4 No. 15, May 1992 p. 1.

37. Robin Wilson, "Flash Point at Rutgers U.," *The Chronicle of Higher Education,* Vol. XLI, No. 24, p. A21.

38. Alan Jenkins, "Domestic Terrorism and Animal Rights Extremists," *Handling Institutional Violence On Campus,* A monograph, International Association of Campus Law Enforcement Administrators, 1993, p. 1.

39. Lawrence J. Fennelly, Charles Lonero, David Neudeck, and Cheryl Vossmer, "Bicycle Theft—Back To Basics," *The Campus Law Enforcement Journal,* Vol. 22, No. 1, January/February 1992, p. 37–40.

40. Bausell, Bausell, and Siegel, p. 45.

41. *Hate Crime Statistics, 1993,* Characteristics of hate crimes in 1993. Summary of hate crime data collection, U.S. Department of Justice, Federal Bureau of Investigation, Washington, D.C.

# Chapter 4

# EFFECTIVE STUDENT AFFAIRS

## INTRODUCTION

A critical element of a safe campus is an institutional commitment to an effective student affairs role in security related issues. The quality of campus life will be determined, in part, by adequate safeguards provided through student affairs policies, procedures, and practices. These should be aimed at promoting personal development and student learning. While student affairs personnel certainly contribute to and support the academic program for which higher education institutions exist, attention to the out-of-class experience is warranted for several very important reasons. In their book, *Involving Colleges*, George Kuh, John Schuh, Elizabeth Whitt and associates, present four important aspects of out-of-class influences:

1) College students spend the majority of their time out of class;
2) A student's peer group exerts considerable influence on how a student spends discretionary time and, thus, on how much time is devoted to study and other educationally purposeful activities;
3) Out-of-class experiences provide opportunities to acquire important skills that are not often addressed in the classroom;
4) Participation in out-of-class activities contributes to a sense of community, a valued constellation of feelings and beliefs in need of attention on many campuses.[1]

Alexander N. Astin, in *What Matters In College?*, examined the impacts of the college experience to include nonacademic aspects. He revealed widespread peer influences on student behavior, political views, and personality development. He found that student-student interaction in general tends to facilitate the student's intellectual and personal development.[2] Much of the time traditional-age students spend out-of-class is with their peers.

Research on college students and their experiences has shown that participation in orientation activities and other social pursuits positively influence both social integration and institutional commitment. Students involved in on-campus, out-of-class experiences are more positive about their college experience. Further, out-of-class activities provide opportunities for development of leadership skills, such as teamwork, decision-making, and planning. Other important issues that are more likely to be addressed in nonacademic settings on campus include social/domestic conflicts, ethical dilemmas, sexuality, drug and alcohol use, and learning to cope with stress. Student participation in such activities as athletic events, parties, concerts, Greek-related rituals, and campus political activism require institutional parameters so that students will successfully mature toward becoming contributing adults.

Today's college students present special challenges for student affairs professionals. Along with the transformation of the campus climate over the past twenty years, the composition of the student body has changed significantly. Whereas students generally resided on campus during the 1950s and 1960s, less than half of today's college students live on campus. More than two-fifths of today's undergraduates are enrolled part-time. Only about half of undergraduates are of traditional college age, eighteen to twenty-three years. There is more diversity. The presence of increasing numbers of students from historically underrepresented racial and ethnic groups emphasizes the need for students to communicate effectively and celebrate differences in cultural heritage, aspirations, and expectations for higher education and personal achievement. Racial incidents on campuses are one manifestation of the significant challenges presented by student diversity.[3] Student affairs officials must address the issue of reestablishing a sense of community on campus with a commitment to appreciating differences. They must deal with the encroachment of a variety of social ills such as guns and violence, alcohol and drug abuse, and racial tensions, all of which threaten this sense of community. On many campuses, most reported incidents of crime are committed by students themselves. Consequently, it is incumbent on student affairs officials to develop effective policies, processes, and strategies which govern student behavior. Today's student affairs leadership must know their students, understand the campus environment, recognize the dynamics of contemporary issues on campus life, and define effective goals for creating a safe campus. Effective policies and practices are essential elements toward ensuring that the quality of life on campus remains reasonably free from internal hostilities and external threats and where students can appreciate diversity and achieve personal and academic goals.

## AN INSTITUTIONAL COMMITMENT

Every college and university should demonstrate a strong commitment to a student affairs role in creating the kind of campus climate which promotes respect for others and encourages a safe and secure environment for students. A top to bottom recognition of campus safety as an institutional priority is needed. This commitment can be evidenced in several ways. Institutional missions and goals should include components which provide for student services/development and foster the creation of a safe campus community for students to pursue their academic, social, and personal objectives. An administrative commitment at the highest level such as the president or chancellor must be articulated through goals, objectives, and organizational design.

The president/chancellor should recognize the importance of student affairs functions and, to that end, appoint a competent chief student affairs officer to fulfill that role. As a practical necessity, presidents must rely substantially on the view of students provided by student affairs officials and faculty. Presidents need student affairs' point of view, and it must be presented squarely and honestly. The province of student affairs on a modern campus is enormous and exceedingly diverse. Each of the many departments in a typical division has a relationship to the president, and each influences his or her perspective by offering a different lens. The president's impressions come from the admissions and financial aid offices, the dean of students, the campus police, health services, the chaplin, counselors, the registrar, the athletic department, the career counseling office, and others. Times have changed. Caught in the vice between demographic trends and economic constraints, most college presidents must make critical decisions based on their perspective of students as shaped by these student affairs professionals.[4] The college president must recognize that campus safety, regardless where the organizational/functional responsibility rests, is a student issue and should be included among student affairs goals and objectives.

Student affairs personnel should develop policies, programs, and practices aimed at ensuring that all students enjoy a threat-free environment. In some cases, this will require special collaborative efforts to join other campus officials in developing effective strategies. Since creating a safe campus is a shared responsibility, student affairs officials should work closely with faculty, security personnel, maintenance staff, and administrators in every division to promote a safe campus climate.

## THE STUDENT AFFAIRS ROLE

The role of the student affairs profession is an emerging one. Historically, the participation of faculty in student services activities has changed from total involvement to detachment. From colonial times through the early 1900s, one role of faculty members was the development of character and values. This was viewed nearly as important as the other two roles—teaching and research. This student development role was due, in part, to the governance function that faculty performed during the early years of American higher education. Academic and social disciplinary activities were the responsibilities of all faculty members. As society became more secular and pluralistic, administrative control was delegated more completely and explicitly to the college president or headmaster. The faculty, instead, gravitated to decision-making primarily within the academic arena. Faculty attitudes toward students became increasingly ambivalent as the faculty member's role changed historically from partners in paternalism to individual entrepreneur. Late in the nineteenth century the appointment of the first "dean of students" signaled the beginning of contemporary diversification of administrative functions in colleges and universities.[5] One of the pioneers in the early student development movement was A.L. Lowell, president of Harvard in 1909. In his inaugural address, he "warned that the recent emphasis upon graduate education and research scholarship was sabotaging the unique functions of the American college. Undergraduates must be helped to develop as well-rounded individuals as well as scholars."[6] This new approach continued to gain momentum through the first half of the nineteenth century. The advent of the GI Bill brought a renewed vigor to the student development philosophy for higher education. This massive funding effort, with its need for academic, personal, and financial advising on nearly every campus in the country called for special student services in unprecedented dimensions.[7] Since that time the student affairs profession along with its diversified services has continued to grow into full blown university divisions.

Today's student affairs role differs little in its focus but has expanded significantly in its scope. The underlying philosophy to the student affairs role is that of educating the "whole person." Student affairs professionals have traditionally adopted a developmental orientation emphasizing responding to the whole person, attending to individual differences and working with students at their levels of development. The National

Association of Student Personnel Administrators, a seventy-five-year-old association with over 1,000 institutional members and 7,000 professional members, has a commitment "to providing services and education that enhance student growth and development. The Association seeks to promote student personnel work as a profession which requires personal integrity, belief in the dignity and worth of individuals, respect for individual differences and diversity, a commitment to service, and dedication to the development of individuals and the college community through education."[8]

Similarly, the *Council for the Advancement of Standards for Student Services/Development Programs* promotes a "whole person" approach to student development. Its standards and guidelines for student development programs offers a holistic approach to the student affairs role (Figure 4.1).[9]

Since the central mission of higher education should be the learning process, it is incumbent on student affairs personnel to direct their student development efforts toward the intellectual and educational process. What may not be apparent or accepted is the role the student affairs can and often does play in relation to the academic program, defined as those activities designed to bring about formal learning, i.e., classroom instruction, laboratories, library study, research, etc. To this list can be added a number of areas to which student affairs can make a special educational contribution such as learning effective citizenship, creating learning communities, developing cultural and artistic environments, teaching acceptance of cultural and racial diversity, orienting students to the collegiate way of life, exploring career and leisure options, and involving students in the fabric of student life.[10]

## STRATEGIES FOR CHANGE

As the higher education industry is facing challenges and change, so is the student affairs component in our nation's colleges and universities. Financial, political, and social pressures on higher education have raised some critical questions for student affairs officials. Can you continue to provide expected levels of programming with anticipated outcomes with less funding and fewer people? Are all of the programs in the student affairs division essential to the mission of the institution? Is there a demand for your services?

Now, more than ever, it is critical that student affairs leaders realistically reexamine their role within the university and the effectiveness of their services to students. Listed below are six recommended strategies which a student affairs division should consider during austere economic times for higher education.[11] These can also be useful in assessing and determining the scope and essential purpose of the student affairs function.

> Stop representing student affairs as a co-curricular unit in competition for academic resources and stress the essentiality of student affairs in the success of students' academic progress.

> Educate faculty members on what it is student affairs does and why it is essential to academia.

> Promote the interface of academic and student affairs as a "seamless experience." Recruitment, retention, matriculation, and success toward graduation are all part of the institutions goals and objectives.

> Involve students as "customers" in the advocacy of student affairs. This will help sustain essential student services.

> Become institutional visionaries by helping other top university leaders recognize that future agendas, issues, and goals will include the need for a strong student affairs role.

> Use hard data to justify the existence and services provided by student affairs. A comprehensive assessment process coupled with regular dissemination of information to key campus officials will help support the need for student affairs.

## MISSION AND GOALS

Each institution and each functional area must develop, review, and disseminate regularly its own mission and specific goals for student affairs. These must be consistent with the nature and goals of the institution. Since institutions vary in size, character, location, and type of students, the organization and nature of student services/development programs will vary. However, the mission of student affairs services in higher education is generally similar from institution to institution. The mission statement and statement of purpose presented in Figure 4.2 was developed in 1992 at Mississippi State University and is typical of those found at most colleges and universities throughout the country. This purpose statement includes a specific component for "safety."

In addition to developing a meaningful mission and purpose for its program, every student affairs organization should establish goals to

**Figure 4.1**

## COUNCIL FOR THE ADVANCEMENT OF STANDARDS FOR STUDENT SERVICES/DEVELOPMENT PROGRAMS—GENERAL STANDARDS: PROGRAM

The overall student services/development program must be (a) purposeful, (b) coherent, (c) based upon or related to theories and knowledge of human development and learning characteristics, and (d) reflective of the demographic and developmental profiles of the student body. Such programs and services must (a) promote student development by encouraging such things as positive and realistic self-appraisal, intellectual development, appropriate personal and occupational choices, clarification of values, physical fitness, the ability to relate meaningfully with others, the capacity to engage in a personally satisfying and effective style of living, the capacity to appreciate cultural and aesthetic differences, and the capacity to work independently and interdependently; (b) assist students in overcoming specific personal, physical, or educational problems or skill deficiencies; and (c) identify environmental conditions that may negatively influence welfare and propose interventions that may neutralize such conditions. The educational experience of students consists of both academic efforts in the classroom and developmental opportunities through student services and development programs. Institutions must define the relative importance of these processes.

which all policies and programs should be directed. These goals should include a safety and security element. This will demonstrate a student affairs commitment to a safe campus environment. Goals also provide a focus for student affairs officials in developing effective programs, strategies, and collaborative efforts. In its annual report the Division of Student Affairs at Jacksonville State University establishes thirteen organizational goals described in Figure 4.3. Goal number six is specifically aimed at creating a safe campus.

## ORGANIZATIONAL DESIGN AND FUNCTIONS

A brief overview of student affairs organizational design and functions will be helpful in understanding the dynamics of an institution-wide approach to creating a safe campus. Any number of organizational models exist. Small colleges often utilize some faculty members in student services work and may also have administrators and staff from several departments performing student affairs functions. Larger, more complex universities tend to adhere to the traditional hierarchical model or

**Figure 4.2**

**MISSION STATEMENT MISSISSIPPI STATE UNIVERSITY**

One of the purposes of higher education is to provide each student with the opportunity for individual development—the opportunity to develop the whole person to include the intellectual, the emotional, the physical and spiritual aspects of one's being. The Division of Student Affairs has as its mission the creation of a campus environment which encourages students to develop autonomy, emotional maturity, values, appreciation of cultural differences, tolerance, and interpersonal skills through meaningful programs and services as well as through interactions with students, faculty and staff. This development which enables students to accept responsible and enlightened citizenship is one of the missions of the University and the central focus of the Division of Student Affairs.

**PURPOSE**

- provide for the safety, health, and well being of students,
- help create a developmental environment for students,
- provide learning experiences outside the classroom,
- help students identify and achieve educational goals,
- provide recreational opportunities for students,
- maximize the University's ability to attract top students and qualified students in appropriate numbers.

pyramid structure with a vice president or dean serving as the chief administrative officer. Some institutions have variations of these within a multidimensional approach. Typical student services functions may be shared among several departments or divisions. Whatever the organizational design, it is important that a strong commitment for a safe campus be shared by those charged with monitoring student success in and out of class. Figure 4.4 illustrates one typical student affairs organizational design at a university with an enrollment of 10,000 students.

The functions and responsibilities assigned to student affairs organizations also vary from institution to institution. Perhaps the most widely accepted listing of traditional student affairs functional areas is found in the Standards and Guidelines for Student Services/Development Programs developed by the Council for the Advancement of Standards for Student Services/Development Programs in 1986. [12] These are as follows:

Academic Advising                    Judicial Programs and Services
Career Planning and Placement        Learning Assistance Programs

**Figure 4.3**

## DIVISION OF STUDENT AFFAIRS
## JACKSONVILLE STATE UNIVERSITY

1. To provide a wide range of wellness programming designed to facilitate the intellectual, emotion, social, occupational, physical and spiritual/ethical dimensions of human growth of the constituents of the university.
2. To provide structured and sequential services enabling the student to make a satisfying adjustment to the college environment and into the world of work upon graduation.
3. To foster and develop personal/social and leadership skills in the collegiate setting that will have transfer value to the student's pursuits beyond higher education.
4. To assist students in the development of skills for planning, conflict resolution, decision-making and personal management.
5. To provide administrative and academic support services to maximize each student's success, satisfaction and persistence.
6. To provide a broad range of public safety programming and security services aimed at improving the quality of life for the campus community.
7. To provide on-going planning, co-ordinative and assessment activities for all student affairs programs.
8. To provide staff development programming and other opportunities for the upgrading of skills for the paraprofessionals, support personnel and professional staff of the division.
9. To support strategic recruitment/marketing and public relations programs in conjunction of the university's enrollment and retention goals.
10. To develop and implement a comprehensive divisional long-range planning process for establishing student affairs priorities and resource allocations and for measuring their effectiveness.
11. To provide programming, staffing and services to foster an understanding and acceptance of different cultures.
12. To develop a comprehensive student affairs' facilities management plan to assess needs, evaluate effective use, and provide for maintenance and renovation.
13. To work cooperatively with faculty and staff in establishing, sharing, and coordinating programs, resources and services.

College Unions
Commuter Student Programs &
Services
Counseling Services
Disabled Student Services
Fraternity and Sorority Advising
Housing and Residential Life Pro.

Minority Student Programs &
  Services
Recreational Sports
Religious Programs
Research and Evaluation
Student Activities
Student Orientation Programs

**Figure 4.4**

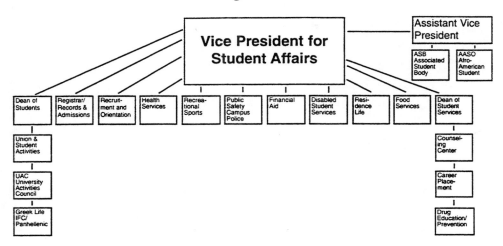

One function not included in this list is that of police and security or public safety. Many colleges and universities place campus public safety under the auspices of the student affairs chief administrative officer. There are some advantages to this approach. Since campus police and security functions are, by and large, directed at creating a safe environment and providing services for students, a natural partnership exists with other student affairs functions. Student activities, social functions, Greek organizations, housing, and judicial processes may all relate in nature and in practice to the role of public safety personnel and services. Whether or not the police and security unit is within the student affairs organization, it is very important that collaborative efforts and strong linkages be established between these two areas so that the quality of campus life will be enhanced.

## POLICIES

Policies and practices within the purview of the student affairs mission should reflect a genuine commitment to ensure campus safety and to regulating student conduct. In this context, "policies and practices" includes a broad range of regulations, rules, activity protocol, procedures, guidelines, and processes. There is a variety of activities which should include provisions for promoting a safe and orderly campus environment. This begins even before students arrive on campus. Perhaps the very first contact the institution makes with prospective students is the "prospective student letter" and accompanying public relations materials. A heightened awareness of campus crime among many parents and prospective college students makes this first contact an important one for introducing the safe campus concept.

The student induction process provides an excellent opportunity for student affairs officials to emphasize the importance of good citizenship and safety responsibilities. Freshmen orientation activities typically offer faculty, staff, and college students the chance to share the institution's academic and social amenities. Through these activities, which are different at each college or university, the bonding process of students to institution and student to student begins. Student affairs staff, public safety officers, counselors, and others can share information related to campus crime and security measures while, at the same time, offering practical tips for personal safety and responsibility. This "gateway" for first-time students affords student affairs officials the prime time to discuss behavioral standards and expectations for social acclimation.

## WRITTEN CONDUCT POLICIES

Written policies may be utilized by colleges and universities to articulate behavior rules and expectations of students. These may be developed by institutional officials or through a collaborative process with students and administrators. While most institutions develop and disseminate student conduct policies, there is a philosophy among some higher education officials that student conduct policies may not always be appropriate for every institution. Some colleges such as Earlham, Grinnele, Mount Holyhoke, and Stanford place few rules and constraints on their students. They prefer student-governed "honor codes." Under these, students determine and maintain community standards. For these honor codes to be effective, students—and their institutions must be committed to principles of fairness, honesty, integrity, and self-governance. In addition, students need to be willing to hold their peers, as well as themselves, accountable for violations of the code. On the other hand, student conduct codes may be seen by students as something for which they have no ownership or the "staff rules."[13]

Written policies related to their new role as "student citizen" should be disseminated to all students upon their arrival to the campus community. These should include a clear explanation of student rights and responsibilities as well as the institutions rights and responsibilities. Figure 4.5 illustrates a typical list of student rights and responsibilities.

These rights and responsibilities are often incorporated into student conduct policies, usually designated as a "student code of conduct" or "honor code". Academic honor codes, when written specifically to with academic dishonesty (i.e., cheating, plagiarism, falsifying class attendance, etc.), may be monitored and enforced by faculty members and/or academic administrators. Some institutions place these responsibilities with student affairs officials. Academic honor codes constitute a statement of trust, student responsibility, and dedication to academic integrity. Such honor systems are usually intended to lack significant structure and often involve student participation in reviewing alleged violations.[14]

Student conduct codes which govern social behavior generally come under the auspices of the student affairs unit. These codes usually describe specific acts of social misconduct. These include a variety of behaviors which are contrary to a safe and orderly campus community. They may include such conduct as assault, weapons possession, theft, vandalism, illegal drugs, hazing, and others. Student conduct codes are usually published in a student handbook and serve to notify students of behaviors which will not be tolerated.

Codes of student conduct should be regularly reviewed to ensure that they meet basic standards: They should be clear, coherent, comprehensive, mutually compatible and enforceable. They must withstand legal scrutiny and challenge. They should be written in common language—not in legalistic terms which are used in criminal and civil proceedings.

Colleges and universities operate within a volatile environment. In order to ensure smooth administration, yet still to fulfill their responsibility of maintaining discipline within an educational environment, colleges and universities are well-advised to establish written conduct or disciplinary codes. For a public college or university, such a written code provides constitutionally required notice to students, faculty, and staff concerning the institution's policies and procedures. It may also ensure against charges of unconstitutional arbitrary action. The private institution may also avoid charges of arbitrary or unfair treatment. A written student conduct code can benefit both public and private institutions, as well as students, by clearly setting forth the terms of the "contract" between the student and the school with respect to disciplinary matters.[15]

**Figure 4.5**

## STUDENTS RIGHTS AND RESPONSIBILITIES

The following statements of rights and responsibilities are not viewed as a final accomplishment of a completed institution, but rather as themes of a direction for a growing and changing educational environment.

I. Students enjoy the same basic rights and are bound by the same responsibilities to respect the rights of others as are all citizens.

   A. It is assumed that the student as a citizen has the rights of freedom of speech, freedom of the press, freedom of peaceful assembly and association, freedom of political beliefs, and freedom from personal force and violence, threats of violence and personal abuse.

   B. The student as a citizen has a right to be considered equally for admission to, employment by and promotion within the campus in accord with the provisions against discrimination in the general law.

   C. It is held that the University is no sanctuary from the general law and, furthermore, that the campus is a community of growth and fulfillment for all, rather than a setting described in the concept of in loco parentis.

II. All students have responsibilities and rights based upon the nature of the educational process and the requirements of the search for truth and its free presentation. These rights and responsibilities include:

   A. Each student has the freedom, dependent upon level of competence, to teach, to learn, and to conduct research and publish findings in the spirit of free inquiry.

   B. Each student has the right to pursue normal curricular and extracurricular activities, including freedom of movement.

   C. Students have the right to expect that records maintained on them contain only information which is reasonably related to the educational purposes or health and safety of the individual or others. Furthermore, it is assumed that the student has the right to protection from unauthorized disclosure of confidential material contained in University records.

   D. Students have the right to reasonable and impartially applied rules, designed to reflect the educational purposes of the institution and to protect the safety of the campus.

   E. Students have the right to recourse if another member of the campus is negligent or irresponsible in the performance of his or her responsibilities or if another member of the campus represents the work of others as his or her own.

**Figure 4.5 Continued**

F. Students who hold opinions about basic policy matters of direct concern to them have the right to have them heard and considered at appropriate levels of the decision-making process. It should be noted that students who have a continuing association with the institution and who have substantial influence have an especially strong obligation to maintain an environment supportive of the rights of others.

III. The University has rights and responsibilities which include but are not limited to the following:
   A. The University has a right and an obligation to present and debate public issues.
   B. The University has a right to prohibit individuals and groups who are not members of the University community from using its name, its finances and its physical operating facilities for commercial or political activities.
   C. The University has the right to prohibit students from using its name, its finances and its physical and operating facilities for commercial activities.

IV. All students have the right to fair and equitable procedures which shall determine the validity of charges that they have violated University regulations.

## CAMPUS JUDICIAL PROCESS

Student conduct codes and academic honor codes should be buttressed by a process whereby alleged violations can be reported and adjudicated in a noncriminal fashion within the university system. A disciplinary process or campus judicial system serves to educate students about their responsibilities, to protect the campus community from unethical and threatening behavior, and to sustain a high degree of integrity with the academic setting. Such processes usually include: authority; disciplinary responsibility; a judicial council; judicial process; disciplinary hearing procedures; and an appeals process. Student affairs officials usually encourage student participation in developing and evaluating student conduct policies and procedures. Students typically play a significant role in administering judicial processes such as membership on judicial councils and appeals courts.

The campus judicial process differs both in purpose and function from the criminal process. A common misunderstanding of many people is that campus judicial proceedings are analogous to civil or criminal proceedings. This is entirely a myth. Colleges and universities are not required to conform to the standards of either civil or criminal law. The campus process is generally thought of as instructional in nature, whereas the criminal process is primarily designed to be punitive, although some legal scholars believe it to be rehabilitative. The procedural functioning of the criminal court system is weighted heavily in favor of protection of the accuseds' rights. Their rights are guaranteed by statutes, such as The Penal Code and Criminal Procedures Law and by the federal and state constitutions. Campus judicial systems are philosophically premised upon protection of the academic community. While the judicial system differs depending on whether the institution is public or private, the protection afforded the accused party are far less comprehensive than those of the criminal system. Likewise, the range of sanction is more restricted and much less severe.[16]

The due process clause of the Fourteenth Amendment mandates that before students at a public institution are sanctioned for misconduct they are entitled to notice of the charge(s) against them and a hearing opportunity. At such hearing the student is entitled to present a defense, produce explanatory testimony, and examine the hearing report. The due process protection granted to students during hearings based solely upon academic infractions are less stringent than those granted during misconduct hearings. Students are entitled only to notice from school authorities that they are deficient in meeting minimum academic performance. The courts reason that they are less qualified to make academic evaluations than are school officials.

Students at private colleges and universities have little procedural protections in disciplinary proceedings. They are not entitled to the hearings or administrative reviews that are guaranteed in the public sector. The protection afforded are contractual in nature arising from the institution's policies and the agreements to attend the institution and abide by its published policies. The courts have traditionally protected students from actions which are clearly arbitrary although still within the private institution's stated policy. Students are held only to a standard of conduct which reasonably sets forth the expectations of the institution. Private college students are not ensured of any First Amendment freedoms except as are agreed upon in the contract they have with the institution.[17]

The administration of student conduct in a university setting is a very complex and challenging task. Today, student conduct issues are guided by legalism and pragmatism. Professionals in judicial affairs are often accused of proceduralism at the expense of addressing the developmental needs of the student. However, if the role of the dean of students or student disciplinary official is effective, student conduct can be one of the most effective means of enhancing the personal development of students. Student judicial officials, student judicial courts, and deans of students are forced to strike a delicate balance between affording the student's basic procedural rights, protecting the community, and creating an opportunity for personal growth and development.[18] The success of creating a safe campus environment hinges, to a significant degree, on the effectiveness of student affairs officials who ensure that sound student conduct policies are enforced through a fair, yet, meaningful judicial process. A wide range of sanctions are at the disposal of the judicial officer and the student judicial court. They include disciplinary probation (academic and/or social), restitution, suspension, expulsion, and special referrals and service.

In addition to sound student conduct policies and effective judicial processes, student affairs officials should endeavor to include safety and security considerations in other aspects of student life. As discussed in Chapter 3, the threats to a safe campus may come "within" by students as well as from "without" by intruders and visitors. When the institution becomes the host to any student event, liability issues become important. Although colleges and universities are generally under no duty to protect students from violent acts of third parties, there are certain special relationships that involve a duty to protect. The landlord-tenant relationship is a well-defined relationship; although "the landlord is no insurer of his tenants' safety, . . . he certainly is no bystander."[19] Not being a bystander includes taking preventive action to minimize predictable risks. Student affairs staff should assess event student activity to determine the risks and develop reasonable and prudent strategies to reduce those risks.

## SUMMARY

The student affairs role in creating a safe campus should be recognized as a high priority among all student affairs officials. Never in the history of higher education has there been such an intense interest on the part of the public, the media, and especially parents about crime on campus. As change agents, advisors, counselors, researchers, educators, and administrators, today's student affairs professionals are concerned with the "whole person" and must recognize the importance of security and safety for student life. The time has come that college and university leaders must understand that ensuring a safe campus environment cannot be the sole responsibility of campus police and security officers. Nor can local law enforcement officials be expected to solve our crime problems on campus. In order to achieve the goal of a safe campus, student affairs professionals will need to examine their policies, processes, and practices for their effectiveness. While there are models of success, each institution's student affairs vice president, dean, or director should encourage his/her staff to explore innovative strategies for addressing their own unique issues and problems.

## ENDNOTES

1. George D. Kuh, John H. Schuh, Elizabeth J. Whitt, and Associates, *Involving Colleges* (San Francisco: Jossey-Bass Publishers, 1991), pp 11 & 12.
2. Alexander W. Astin, *What Matters In College?: Four Critical Years Revisited,* (San Francisco: Jossey-Bass Publishers, 1993), pp. 104, 185, and 364.
3. Kuh, 1991, p. 15.
4. Margaret J. Barr and Associates, *The Handbook of Student Affairs Administration,* (San Francisco: Jossey-Bass Publishers, 1993), p. 85.
5. Ursula Delworth, Gary R. Hanson and Associates, *Student Services: A Handbook for the Profession,* (San Francisco: Jossey-Bass Publishers, 1980), pp. 14–19.
6. John S. Brubacher and Willis Rudy, *Higher Education In Transition,* 3rd ed. (New York: Harper and Row, 1976), pp. 335–336.
7. Delworth, p. 22.
8. National Association of Student Personnel, (Washington, D.C., 1993), Member Handbook, 1993–1994, p. 15.
9. Council for the Advancement of Standards for Student Services/Development Programs, 1986, p. 5.
10. Paul A. Boland, Louis C. Stametakos, and Russell R. Rogers, *Reform In Student Affairs: A Critique of Student Development,* (Greensboro, North Carolina: ERIC Counseling and Student Services Clearinghouse, 1994), p. 96.
11. Roger A. Ballou, "On-Campus Strategies to Sustain Our Profession", NASPA Forum, November 1995, pp. 3 and 5.
12. Council for the Advancement of Standards for Student Services/Development Programs.
13. Kuh, Schuh, Whitt, et. al. p. 137.
14. Ibid, p. 139.
15. Edward N. Stones and Cathy Cerminara, "Harassing the 'Spirit of Insubordi-

nation': A Model Student Disciplinary Code", *Journal of College and University Law,* February, 1990, Vol. 17, No. 2, pp. 91 and 92.

16. Charles F. Carletta, "Campus Student Judicial Process: Public vs. Private," Presented at the 16th Annual Law and Higher Education Conference, Clearwater Beach, Florida, February 12–14, 1995.

17. Ibid.

18. Diane M. Waryold, "Campus Assault Scenario: Student Judicial Officer," Presented at the 15th Annual Law and Higher Education Conference, Clearwater Beach, Florida, February 13–16, 1994.

19. Barr, p. 277.

# Chapter 5

# EFFECTIVE POLICE AND SECURITY SERVICES

## INTRODUCTION

A critical element of a safe campus is the provision of effective police and security services. College and university officials committed to ensuring that students are afforded a reasonably safety and secure campus environment should recognize the importance of adequate law enforcement and security. To the dismay of many academicians and higher education administrators the college campus is no longer a safe haven from the ills of the real world. Today's campus has become vulnerable to many of the same threats that plague our communities. The reality of our modern society to include its academic institutions is that there are few places where one can assume to be safe. However, students should expect some measure of protection from threats outside the institution as well as those perpetrated within the campus community, often by other students. University administrators should do no less for students than government officials do for their citizenry. They should provide effective public safety services aimed at creating a safe campus and fostering a sense of security among students, faculty, staff, and visitors.

## THE EVOLUTION OF CAMPUS PUBLIC SAFETY

Any enlightened discussion of campus public safety should be predicated on an understanding of its brief history. For sure, there are many and varied perceptions about campus safety and security services. Some of the more errant notions came from images of past practices. First, for clarification for this discussion the terms campus public safety, campus police, campus security and campus law enforcement are used interchangeably with similar meaning except where specifically differentiated.

The beginning of the modern campus police force can be traced back to the school maintenance staff or faculty chairman of the school grounds. Their major attention was focused on physical needs such as building construction, the provision of heat, waste disposal, fire prevention, and protecting property from trespassers or straying animals. Neal states, "In different eras and on different campuses his forerunner was the janitor, or the watchmen, or the faculty chairman of the grounds committee, or in some cases the lineage can be traced directly to the president of the institution. While campus living is intended to foster student learning through well-planned, safe, integrated, and coherent educational experiences, crime and threats to personal tranquility can diminish the anticipated outcomes and impacts. Most higher education housing professionals realize that many and perhaps most of the incidents of victimization occurring on their campuses occur in their residence halls, primarily because that is where most students on a residential campus are at night and on weekends and it is where alcohol is most often consumed.[1] Apartments, fraternity and sorority houses, and other forms of residence are no exception to this premise. Students dwelling on campus and in nearby housing units may face higher risks of becoming victims of property crimes than the national average. This is due, in part, to the factor.

In all probability, campus safety/security had its formal beginning in 1894 when the Yale Campus Police was established. Because of frequent conflicts between Yale students and townspeople that often developed into full-scale riots, two New Haven police officers were hired by Yale as campus police officers. These officers retained their sworn authority as city officers, a situation that has existed for Yale officers to this day. One of these first officers, William Weiser, was appointed chief. Chief Weiser wrote a book in 1914, entitled *Yale Memories,* in which he stated that his department's most important function was to "protect the students, their property, and University property."[2] While Yale established a police department in 1894, this was the exception rather than the rule.

During the early 1900s, there was little need for campus police or security forces and most colleges and universities depended entirely upon the local police to handle any criminal violations and campus disruptions. Most matters involving student misbehavior were handled "internally" through the dean of students' office.

During the 1920s, the watchman or guard appeared as the predominant approach to campus safety. Historically, these watchmen, who were usually older retired men and employed only at night and on weekends, were attached to the maintenance or physical plant department. Their main concern was with the protection of college property. These watchmen were given no training as law enforcement officers and were not expected to perform as such. Their chief functions were to determine the security of buildings at night and on weekends (e.g., closing windows, locking and unlocking doors, and other duties to protect property) and "patrol" the campus in order to detect fire hazards, check boilers, detect leaky pipes and otherwise perform preventive maintenance duties. With the repeal of Prohibition in the early 1930s, the watchman-guard gradually began to take on other functions dealing with the enforcement of rules and regulations governing student conduct.[3]

While the watchman-guard type approach was common until the 1950s, there were a few colleges and universities that established police oriented safety/security departments. One such institution was the University of Maryland. In 1936, after the rotation of many Maryland State Troopers temporarily assigned to the campus at College Park, two volunteered for permanent duty at the university and subsequently were hired by the university as campus police officers.[4]

It was during the decade of the fifties that university administrators began to recognize the need for a more organized protective force on campus. This was brought on by the problems created by increasing growth and consequent complexities of the campus. Increases in enrollment, potential increases in behavioral incidents, expansion of the physical plant, increases in motor traffic, and problems related to parking led to an awareness for some semblance of police presence on campus. Consequently, at the beginning of the 1950s, retired law enforcement officials were hired as campus "cops" and often patterned campus safety departments after models used in municipal settings. Usually, the "police" authority was still limited to detection of crime, physical security functions, and notification of local police authorities in the event of necessary arrests or other formal police action.[5]

In 1953, the Northeastern College and University Security Association was formed by a group of campus security administrators in the Northeast to foster professionalism and the exchange of information. Soon to follow this effort was the formation of the National Association of College and University Traffic and Security Directors in 1958, which is now the International Association of College and University Law Enforcement Administrators. This association presently has over 800 institutional members. These associations were clear indications that the once campus watchmen-guards were becoming organized and developed into more professionally oriented safety officers.[6]

However, it was not until the tumultuous sixties when disorder and crime were introduced to the academic community that college administrators realized the inadequacy of their campus "law" and, at the same time, became dissatisfied with the local police attitudes and methods. Subsequently, administrators concerned not only with students' needs, peace, and safety, but also with autonomy of law enforcement responsibilities on campus, recognized the time for a change of priorities and the need for a new direction which would create a more professional police/security department on campus. The concept of hiring former municipal and county police officers began to be less popular.[7]

During the 1970s, campus security began to be programmed to meet student problems and needs. It emphasized a low-key but highly professional approach utilizing well-trained young officers who were either enrolled in college degree programs or who had already achieved a degree. These officers were often attired in blazer-slacks outfits bearing the college seal and department name instead of the police-type uniforms of the former watchmen-guards. Professional degree-holding safety and security administrators were very much in demand to head these departments. Security directors, who once answered to the head of the physical plant, were now often reporting to the president and vice-president. In a 1968 survey of 120 campus safety and security directors, Nielson reported that less than one-half of all respondents still reported to the physical plant director. Among this group, from 28 percent to 60 percent, depending on the category, advocated a change to reporting to a vice-president.[8] In a 1985 dissertation study, 67 percent of campus police safety directors reported to a vice president while only 22 percent reported to the director of physical plant. This trend would suggest that the role of watchman-guard with its property protection orientation is changing to one of a more professional police and "people" orientation.[9]

## AN INSTITUTIONAL COMMITMENT

There should be a commitment by boards of regents, college chancellors, presidents, and other top administrators to provide adequate security personnel for the campus community. Certainly the type of security services will vary depending on the particular needs and circumstances of the institution. Authority, number of officers, jurisdiction, and responsibilities are among the variables for consideration by campus administrators. Whether contract security, local police, or institutional police/

security is used will be determined by the unique requirements of the institution. What is important is to provide an adequate level of security capable of reasonable crime prevention functions and reliable enough to respond to calls for emergency assistance.

Expectations for a safe campus environment have increased for all types of institutions, and recent federal legislation (see discussion in Chapter 9) requiring that crime data be reported has heightened the awareness of the campus police role. Under the Crime Awareness and Campus Security Act of 1990, colleges and universities are also required to establish certain security policies and procedures which include an important role for on-campus police or security personnel. Liability concerns alone should compel administrators to place a high priority on the provision of adequate police/security services.

Generally, colleges and universities have imputed by law a duty to warn and also a duty to provide reasonably adequate security protection. This duty may arise in two ways: either under a "negligence" theory based on tort law, or upon a breach of contract theory, based upon some assurance that the institution has given pertaining to protection or safety. Security protection includes a number of measures such as locks, fences, lights, police officers, and security guards. Adequacy of police protection has been an issue in several court cases. While the courts have been hesitant to impose any duty to guarantee that, through policing, crime does not occur, a duty to provide police protection for campus residents could arise in some circumstances.[10] For example, in Jesik v. Maricopa Community College, the Arizona Supreme Court ruled that a campus security guard's failure to act may have been a factor in the shooting death of another student.[11]

While tort law imposes no duty to provide adequate security protection in a given situation, it is possible for higher education institutions to create their own duty. Institutions which claim their campuses to be safe and secure may create a contractual relationship with its students. Such assurances are often found in promotional literature, brochures, and catalogues.

These liability concerns should cause college and university administrators to take a close look at the scope and quality of their institutions police/security operation. They should demonstrate a strong and clear commitment which supports an effective campus police and security presence.

College presidents should play a key role in determining the nature and effectiveness of campus law enforcement and security. The president should also actively participate in guiding campus police policy by a simple announcement that justice is to be served, even if the institution is consequently embarrassed or otherwise diminished. Campus police officials must understand that they are to do the right thing and expect consistent support from campus administrators. Unfortunately, too many presidents, administrators, and faculty members do not understand or appreciate the important role of campus police and security personnel.

Peter Likins, Ph.D., president of Lehigh University, is a college president who has, perhaps, a unique perspective about the role of campus police. He states:

> A campus police department has a delicate task, combining citizenship education with the enforcement of the laws and regulations that preserve order in the campus community. Probably few people appreciate the difficulty of these responsibilities, including institutional presidents.

> Our police must deal with students who can be in their ugliest states: either drunk or angry at some imposed constraint. They also must act perfectly in times of genuine, life threatening crisis. And because they represent the authority of the institution, and indeed the president, they must be unfailingly kind, helpful, cheerful, and positive in their attitudes. That is a great deal to ask, particularly of men and women who may sometimes resent the presumptions of students preparing to take their place as leaders of society. Yet, we do ask for all these qualities and more, because we must. The least we can do is demonstrate our respect and appreciation for the work of the campus police.[12]

## ORGANIZATIONAL CONSIDERATIONS

As mentioned in an earlier discussion on the history of campus police, campus public safety departments were historically located within physical facilities operations or maintenance departments. Typically, the chief or director reported to a maintenance supervisor or other lower-level manager within the institution. However, with the expansion of its services and responsibilities over the past three decades, campus police and security personnel have a much broader role. Since their functions may now include student safety, parking and traffic enforcement, fire safety, law enforcement, criminal investigations, and other more traditional public safety services, many campus police operations have been assigned to report to vice presidents. Certainly, the organizational position of campus public safety continues to vary from one institution to another. Yet there is a marked trend upward with the organizational structure of the institution.

Increasingly, campus public safety operations have been placed with divisions of student affairs. Campus police chiefs and public safety directors who are assigned to vice presidents of student affairs generally report favorably to this arrangement. They cite the positive relations and direct participation with officials on common issues involving student activities and student conduct (or misconduct).

Another common organizational configuration for campus public safety places police and security services within the business affairs division. Typically, this is also the location of physical facilities. While this division may be more "physical plant" oriented than student-focused, an assiduous vice president will recognize the importance of student security issues and encourage strong linkages between campus police and student affairs officials.

Whatever the organizational placement within the institution, public safety directors should be placed at a level which will afford the status and access which allows him/her to communicate with key officials across divisional lines as well as with vice presidents and even the president when appropriate. There should be no more than one level or position between the campus public safety director and the president of the institution. If the law enforcement/security functions must report through several bureaucratic layers, the reports and information tend to be filtered and, thus, diminished.

## LAW ENFORCEMENT VS. SERVICE

Campus public safety departments, like municipal police agencies, have two broad roles to fulfill: law enforcement and service. It is estimated that most local police spend approximately ninety percent of their time on service activities and the remainder on strict law enforcement functions. Law enforcement functions include arrests, criminal investigations, response to criminal incidents, and the apprehension of suspects. Campus police officers with a law enforcement orientation tend to respond to incidents with a similar approach as do municipal police officers. Service activities include duties such as traffic control, assisting motorists, taking reports, security, routine patrol, crime prevention and many other nonlaw enforcement task. Officers with a service orientation will tend to take a more nonpolice approach to most situations when possible. Under these definitions, most campus police agencies probably devote more than 95 percent of their time and effort toward service to the campus community and very little time to strict law enforcement duties. However, the law enforcement role of campus public safety organizations is often an issue of considerable confusion and controversy among some university officials.

While many campus public safety agencies now resemble municipal police departments in organizational structure, uniforms, policies, procedures, and overall image, there exists a marked difference in terms of approach and the emphasis on service. Campus police departments generally stress service to their student customers. This is appropriate since a primary objective of higher education institutions is service. This philosophy is embodied in the Florida State University Public Safety Department's General Order which states: "While the principal objective of the Department is the maintenance of a safe and secure physical environment, it is necessary to recognize that particularly with service as its main product, the goals of a public safety organization must continuously be responsive to the needs and problems of the community it serves.[13]

While it is generally agreed by university administrators and campus public safety officials that the service role should be predominant within the campus community, there is less agreement among these officials as to the extent of the law enforcement role. Some college presidents prefer to relegate campus police to mere night watchmen while others recognize the significance and necessity of maintaining a police presence on campus. This role perception conflict has existed for years.

In the last three decades, campus public safety officers in most public universities have been empowered with the same sworn police authority as any other peace officer (i.e., municipal, county, state). Subsequently, these safety officers may perceive themselves as law enforcement oriented and function accordingly. The director of campus public safety, who is usually a veteran police officer, may tend to support this orientation. Often this law enforcement orientation conflicts with the expectations of the central administration, since many college presidents and their administrative subordinates perceive the role of the campus public safety division to be more service and security oriented.

Such a conflict in perceptions of the role of the campus public safety department could have significance in several ways. It could result in the campus public safety department failing to meet the objectives of the institution's mission and goals. It could result in a lack of harmony and understanding between the director and his/her direct supervisor. It could result in administration's lack of support for the public safety department's efforts. It could determine what kinds of programs, personnel, training and procedures the public safety department requires. Also, with no clear, university-wide philosophy and policy on the role of campus public personnel embraced by the director, the safety officers could experience frustration. Finally, the kind of service that the academic community receives from the campus public safety department could be affected.

The following recommendations are offered to reduce this role conflict and to improve public safety services:

1. A needs-assessment study should be conducted by colleges with participation by administrators, faculty and students to determine what public safety services are needed and what image they perceive the safety department to need.
2. Philosophy, policies and procedures should be developed jointly by the administration and the campus public safety department in keeping with the results of a campus-wide needs-assessment study regarding the role of the campus public safety department.
3. A clear and structured process of communication should be established for the campus public safety director and his/her immediate supervisor for the purpose of clarifying philosophies, policies, procedures and objectives of the campus safety department.
4. A survey should be conducted by the institution to find out how other colleges and universities deal with criminal and misconduct incidents and what kinds of services their safety/security department provides.

## LEADERSHIP

Perhaps the key to providing effective police and security services to the campus community is an assiduous leader. The head of the campus public safety department must have a unique understanding of higher education's mission and the role of public safety within that mission. This individual should have a proper perspective with regard to balancing the enforcement of the law and meeting the special needs of students during this developmental period of their lives. This perspective must be shared with every employee within the public safety organization through role orientation activities.

Even though campus police/security organizations operate within a larger academic/collegial environment where "collaboration" and "shared decisions" are acceptable approaches, the police department too often maintains a rigid, hierarchical management style. It is almost as if amid decades of research and change in management and leadership theory, campus police organizations, like their municipal counterparts, have resisted and have remained stuck in an early 20th century rut. Despite innovations and improvements in campus policing, the campus police department's management approach has changed very little.

Today's typical campus police organization, whether it serves a larger urban campus, a small private college, a two-year institution, or a mid-size regional university, closely resembles the military model. In light of American law enforcement's historical development this is understandable. Perhaps the most important similarity is their authority to employ forces to maintain order. In emergencies both require near automatic and unquestionable acceptance of authority by their members. As a result, law enforcement has traditionally been founded on this military model of authority. This rigid rank and "top-down" authority and decision-making approach extends beyond emergency circumstances to everyday, routine management operations. In fact, men and women drawn to the profession generally hold authority-based values.

The impact of individually held, authority-based values on the profession is enormous, giving it a military look, philosophy, and atmosphere. Such military-based authority model views authority as residing with the chief executive of the organization; that is, authority that originates from and is vested solely in a central official. Police agencies, whether campus, municipal, or others, are hierarchically organized to maximize central control over rank-and-file behavior. Moreover, as bureaucratic entities, formal legal rationality and strong division of labor are integral aspects of police organizations.

Perhaps the biggest stumbling block to the acceptance and accomplishment of change may be police leadership. While significant progress has been achieved in more highly educated police leaders, many police executives still lack the necessary skills and/or the tenacity to initiate sweeping organizational changes. Many have a traditional mentality about power and are reluctant to share it.

Today's campus police organization has an increasing number of highly educated, well trained officers who are capable of shedding the top-down, authority-based approach and accepting change. In fact, many of these individuals are highly motivated and creative and easily become stagnant and discouraged when their ideas and initiatives are suppressed by a rigid organizational structure. Consequently, performance levels often drop, morale is low, and the organization's effectiveness, in terms of achieved objectives and image, is reduced.

Essentially, the concept and implementation of empowerment is yet to be embraced by most police organizations. Police organizations in general present a unique challenge to effecting this strategy. However, when the principles of empowerment are examined along with successful examples of implementation both in the business/industry field and in police organizations, the challenge may seem less difficult and more inevitable.

Successful empowerment or stewardship in any organization will require effective leadership. Leading is a responsibility, and the effectiveness of this responsibility is reflected in the attitudes of the led.

How can empowerment work in existing military-oriented, campus police/security organizations? There is no reason to believe it will not work and, in fact, significantly improve these organizations. First of all, the notion should be dispelled which concern some police leaders: empowerment does not decrease the leader's power or authority. The reverse is true. By allowing individuals within the organization to share in decision-making on issues and activities affecting them, and "their" organization, the leader's power, influence, support, and authority are enhanced. Furthermore, the leader increases the "fellowship" among employees when they believe there is a genuine partnership or ownership in the organization.

The key to empowering the police environment is leadership. It is up to progressive campus police leaders to give serious considerations to the benefits derived from implementing a participative management strategy. It may be done gradually and it may be done in some limited approach. The leader will find both position and authority are strengthened, the organization healthier and more productive, and, most important, the people who make up the organization will enjoy being a part of it. This shared accountability coupled with shared authority will create the entrepreneurial environment necessary to thrive in today's campus community.

An effective leader will also focus the attention of the campus public safety department on the student as customer. Whether it is called total quality management (TQM), community policing, or policing by objectives, campus police and security officers must understand that students are their customers and it is for their business of education that the institution exists. In a sense, campus police are just as important to customer satisfaction as are faculty members and student affairs personnel. Every policy, every procedure, and every activity should be developed with the students foremost in mind. The director of the campus police or security organization should continually orient employees toward this philosophy until it becomes an "institutionalized" part of the organization and culture.

## SPECIAL POLICE AND SECURITY SERVICES

University public safety organizations, whether as small as a five-member force or as large as one hundred officers, generally provide similar services to the campus communities they serve. Certainly, the scope and types of services will vary depending on such factors as the size of the institution, the kind of academic program offered, the relationship to local police, and the authority of the campus public safety officers. The similarities among campus police/security departments far exceed their differences. Typically, they wear traditional military-style uniforms, represent authority, perform crime prevention and security duties, and are responsible to some degree for parking and traffic management. A brief descriptive list which offers an overview of these services follows.

### Law Enforcement

Most universities, public and private, provide some law enforcement-related services. Even though some institutions are not authorized to employ sworn police officers, their security forces usually provide at least quasi-law enforcement services (i.e., enforcement of minor violations of law and/or institutional rules, detaining trespassers, apprehending suspects for local police, etc.,). For example, a nonsworn campus security officer may apprehend a nonstudent for criminal trespassing, detain him until local police officers arrive, and obtain an arrest warrant through the local court magistrate. Hundreds of colleges and universities do, in fact, provide trained, commissioned police officers on campus. These officers are capable of performing the same basic law enforcement duties as municipal police officers. It is advantageous to have campus police with this capability in that it affords the institution more autonomy while, at the same time, enhancing on-campus security and emergency response.

Whatever the type of institution, few are immune from circumstances and incidents that will require a law enforcement response by public safety officers. Criminal activity exists on all campuses. University administrators cannot ignore this fact and must be willing to respond accountably in order to ensure the safety of students. It is important, therefore that university officials recognize the need to provide an effective public safety operation capable of either performing law enforcement tasks when required or be able to summons local police to assist in enforcing laws on campus.

## Facilities Security

Every institution of higher education should have an effective security system and security measure to protect its students and employees as well as its property. While campus police and security officers are an indispensable component of facilities security, the use of electronic security has increased dramatically in recent years as technology has progressed. A multiplicity of electronic security systems are available. A major part of facilities security involves access control. Unauthorized entry into campus buildings has plagued university officials for many years. The use of security personnel coupled with electronic equipment is found to be effective on most campuses. Facilities security is an important function of the campus public safety department and often involves the security of a wide range of facilities to include libraries, science labs, technology facilities, and housing units.

## Special Event Security

Campus police and security departments routinely provide special security functions for a wide variety of on-campus events. These include intercollegiate sporting events such as football, basketball, baseball, soccer, and other sports. These events often generate crowds on campus as large as near 100,000 people. Other special events which create a demand on campus public safety officials include large rock music concerts, homecoming activities, commencement ceremonies, political rallies, and other special emphasis activities. These events call for additional security personnel, increased traffic control, and extensive management efforts for planning and coordination.

## Parking Management

Parking on campus is significant for many higher education institutions—both large and small, rural and urban. Since most colleges and universities were built in the pre-automobile era or in the early years of the auto industry, campus streets and parking areas were not initially constructed to handle the volume of vehicles resulting from the enrollment explosion of the 1960s. Consequently, parking on many campuses is a premium. The management of a campus parking system to include vehicle registration, planning, parking assignments, and parking enforcement has become a major role for university officials. This function is most often assigned to the campus police/security unit but sometimes is separately assigned to a special parking unit with the director reporting to a vice president.

## Crime Prevention

The prevention of criminal activity on today's college campus is an underlying theme for all campus public safety services such as law enforcement and building security. However, many institutions with larger police/security departments (i.e., twenty or more offices) have designated a special unit with specially trained individuals to focus on crime prevention efforts beyond the usual routine patrol and building security tasks. Today, campus crime prevention has become somewhat sophisticated with policies, procedures, programs, literature, videos, and special activities all geared toward citizen participation and a "shared responsibility" philosophy. Crime prevention is also a foundation piece for the "community policing" strategy. Crime prevention activities will be presented throughout several other discussions which follow.

## Fire Safety

From the early years of higher education during the 1700s and early 1800s, fire safety has been a concern for campus security whether that be the night watchman of yesteryear or today's campus police officer. Their presence on an around-the-clock basis offers practical reasoning that campus police and security officers should at least monitor buildings for not only intrusion but also for damage due to fire or other threats. Beyond their monitoring tasks, many campus public safety departments are responsible for checking fire alarms systems, conducing routine fire drills, recommending fire safety systems and devices, and conducting campus-wide fire safety education programs. Some institutions, however, have assigned these functions to separate units devoted to general environmental safety to include fire safety. The responsible unit should also coordinate fire protection and fire fighting services with local fire department officials who may also assist campus personnel with fire safety activities.

## Special Services

Often campus public safety departments become the "catch all" of a wide variety of tasks and responsibilities. Some of these are traditional assignments while others have been more recently added. The following list, while not all inclusive, represents some of the special services provided by many campus police and security departments:

Key Control
Student I.D. Management
Lost and Found Property
Money Escorts
Female Security Escorts
Disaster Preparedness/Coordination
Victim's Advocacy Programs

Bicycle Registration
V.I.P. Security
Assist Motorists
Raising Flags
Severe Weather Monitoring/Notification
Parade/March Escorts
Alcohol/Drug Abuse Programs

## THE CAMPUS POLICE ROLE IN COMMUNITY POLICING

In an effort to more effectively serve their communities, police agencies across the country are modifying their approach to the traditional "protect and serve" approach which has been, by and large, a reactive approach. The current movement in law enforcement is a community-oriented or community-based form of policing. It is characterized as proactive, decentralized, and creative. It hinges on the expanded role of individual police officers working with the community to establish a partnership that facilitates problem solving.[14] This approach to campus crime prevention will be discussed in Chapter 6.

# SUMMARY

Effective police and security services are essential components of creating a safe campus. There should be a strong commitment by top university officials to develop and maintain a public safety operation which includes professional leadership, well-trained personnel, and meaningful programs. The college president should clearly articulate his/her support to the police/security organizations and this support should be embraced among other administrators, faculty, and staff. Campus public safety should no longer be relegated to the lowest level within the institutional organization, but be promoted to a status equal to its importance today in creating a safe campus.

An effective campus police or security organization calls for strong, progressive leadership which understands the unique campus community. The "top cop" should also understand the institution's mission and objectives and be able to translate these into appropriate goals services for the police/security organization. He/she must recognize the importance of shared decision making, especially within the academic, collegial climate of a university. Proper role orientation for all police/security personnel is essential for effective delivery of service to the campus community.

The multiplicity of services performed by campus police and security forces is significant to the campus community. Unlike their municipal counterparts, effective campus public safety operations focus on much more than just law enforcement and traffic control. Campus police should emphasize the service role and demonstrate this through community policing efforts. This will require a customer service philosophy among campus police/security officers as well as students. These efforts will enhance crime prevention programs and reduce the risks of crime and violence which threaten our campuses.

# ENDNOTES

1. Robert E. Neal, "A History of Campus Security: Early Origins," *Campus Law Enforcement Journal,* Vol. 10, No. 28 (1980); p. 28.
2. John W. Powell, *Campus Security and Law Enforcement* (Boston, Massachusetts: Butterworth, Inc., 1971), p. 55.
3. Diane C. Bordner and David M. Petersen, *Campus Policing: The Nature of University Police Work* (New York, New York: University Press of America, 1983), p. 34.

4. Eugene Sides, "Policing the Campus: Responsibilities of A University Police Department," *The Police Chief,* 50, (1983): 69–70.
5. Bordner and Petersen, *Campus Policing,* p. 38.
6. David Nichols, *The Administration of Public Safety In Higher Education* (Springfield, Illinois: Charles C. Thomas, 1987), p. 10.
7. Bordner and Petersen, *Campus Policing,* p. 11.
8. Swen C. Nielson, *General Organizational and Administrative Concepts for University Police* (Springfield, Illinois: Charles C. Thomas, 1971), p. 52.
9. David Nichols, A Doctoral Dissertation entitled "Perceptions of the Role of Campus Public Safety Departments By Safety Directors and their Immediate Supervisors, University of Alabama, 1985, p. 55.
10. Michael Clay Smith and Richard Fossey, *Crime On Campus: Legal Issues and Campus Administration* (Phoenix, Arizona: American Council On Education: Oryx Press, 1995), p. 60.
11. Ibid, p. 60, (125 Ariz. 543, 611 P. 2d 547, 1980).
12. Margaret Barr and Associates, *The Handbook of Student Affairs Administration,* Chapter 6, "The President: Your Master or Your Servant," by Peter Likins.
13. Florida State University Department of Public Safety, Department Philosophy, General Order 85-1, 1985.
14. Paul Lang and Bryan C. Carver, "Community Policing: A Case For Campus Police," *Community Policing On Campus,* (Hartford, Connecticut: International Association of Campus Law Enforcement Administrators, 1995), p. 2.
15. Bureau of Justice Assistance, *Understanding Community Policing: A Framework For Action,* Washington, D.C., 1994, p. 23.

# Chapter 6

# COMMUNITY POLICING ON CAMPUS

## INTRODUCTION

C reating a safe campus requires continuous assessment of what works and what does not work. In responding to the steady rise in campus crime for nearly thirty years, institutions have, by and large, followed traditional strategies used by municipal police agencies. These include routine vehicle patrol, enhanced communications capabilities, and police-made crime prevention programs. Whether these methods worked or not, campus police officials kept using them year after year because, in part, their municipal counterparts did. This is not to imply that some campus police/security leaders did not employ innovative strategies here and there. What it does say is that, despite substantial increases in serious incidents of murder, rape, robbery, and aggravated assaults, many campus police/security officers continued to ride aimlessly around campus in their well-equipped patrol cars. More officers, better equipment, and more money made little difference in reducing crime on campus. This was almost directly parallel to circumstances in cities and communities across the nation.

Fortunately there are indications that things are looking up. For the first time in nearly four decades, American policing is undergoing some fundamental changes which hold promise for easing the crime problem. In essence, policing is being redefined. Some have described this new approach a "back to the future" concept that harrows some of its basic elements from the early years in policing, nearly a century ago. Community policing or community-oriented policing as it is called, has gained momentum in recent years as police and community leaders search for more effective ways to promote public safety and to enhance the quality of life in their neighborhoods. Chiefs of police, sheriffs, and other policing officials are currently assessing what changes in orientation, organization, and operations will allow them to benefit the communities they serve by improving the quality of the services they provide. Community policing encompasses a variety of philosophical and practical approaches and is still evolving rapidly. Community policing strategies vary depending on the needs and responses of communities served.

Just as municipal law enforcement agencies throughout the country have moved towards community policing as a means of addressing the changing society of the 1990s, university police and security agencies have had to address the same changes in their campus communities. While some would postulate that campus police/security forces have traditionally operated in a community-based police mode, this has generally not been the case. The organizational and philosophical transformation required for true community policing on campus involves a strong commitment by college and university officials, especially campus police/security directors. It is not an instantaneous occurrence, but change that occurs over time and through concerted efforts. University police and security officials can become more effective and can better accomplish crime prevention goals through a commitment to community policing.[1]

## HISTORICAL PERSPECTIVE

Community police or community-oriented policing has gained national attention and has become very popular since the early 1990s. Virtually every criminal justice journal magazine, and textbook now addresses this redefined policing strategy. Increasingly, local government leaders are calling for this new direction for their police agencies. Campus police publications, professional conferences, and training seminars inevitably include topics related to community policing.

The community policing phenomenon that is currently sweeping the country has deep roots that extend all the way back to the early 1800s with Britain's Sir Robert Peel. In 1829, Peel founded the London Metropolitan Police Force on some innovative and sound principles. These principles form the basis of many American law enforcement practices today. Peel espoused the importance of the police relying on the public (or community) for their approval, support, and respect. He stated: " . . . the police are the public and the public are the police."[2] In fact, the early years of America's history, police officers functioned with a community oriented approach. They typically performed night watchmen duties, walked beats, provided a wide variety of services, and, most importantly, knew and were known by neighborhood residents. Other than a few well-known riots and urban crime problems, crime in America remained insignificant throughout most of the nineteenth century. Then, the populations grew with immigration, the industrial revolution cranked up, and the automobile became the principal mode of transportation. The environment changed, cities changed, communities changed, and so did American policing. By the early 1900s, police leaders began what would become the modern professional era of policing. Technology, sophisticated communications, and improved police training and methods were promoted by police executives, presidential commissions, newly organized police professional associations, and the public. Despite the significant advancement, a new and alarming wave of crime occurred in the 1960s. The civil rights movement, Vietnam, campus unrest, explosion of illegal drug use, and street violence all seemed to converge during the decade of the sixties. The police were simply unprepared to deal with the complexities of this social change of such radical proportions. Their modern technology, state-of-the-art equipment, and professionalism served only to react to problems which had much deeper roots. The source of America's problems were to be found in broken homes, poor neighborhoods, racial tensions, social isolation, and undisciplined schools.

Several important reforms during the late 1960s and early 1970s were launched in an attempt to turn the tide on society's crime wave. One of the earliest articulations of what would later evolve into community policing philosophy can be found in an innovative program in San Francisco in 1962. The San Francisco Police Department established a specialized unit based on the concept that "police would help to reduce crime by reducing despair—by acting as a social service agency to ameliorate some of the difficulties encountered by minority group persons."[3] This effort struggled from the outset. Members of the specialized unit were unsure of the mission and did not understand which appropriate methods should be used in serving the minority community. The unit also faced the dilemma of how to maintain its police identity and, at the same time, effectively relate to the minority population. Eventually, the relationship of trust between the unit and the community led to formal complaints of misconduct against other police officers, sealing the unit's alienation from the mainstream of the department. The program soon perished in the politically charged environment it inadvertently helped to create.[4]

In the 1970s a new strategy emerged—team policing. The team policing concept assigned responsibility for a certain geographic area to a team of police officers who would learn the neighborhood, its people, and its problems—much like the old cop on the beat. Different American cities tried various forms of team policing, but none ever got beyond the limited "pilot-project" stage, and all eventually fell by the wayside.[5]

Despite these efforts, America's crime problems continued to exacerbate into the 1980s with gang violence, more illegal drug-related crimes, carjackings, juvenile violence, disrupted schools, and random killings. Faced with the dilemma of becoming totally ineffective to turn the tide of this violent crime wave, police leaders recognized that different approaches were necessary. Thus, they turned to the community for help. Consequently, through research, government support, and police leadership, partnerships between police agencies and a variety of community constituencies have now been formed in an effort to restore peace and safety to every neighborhood and every community in this country. Some believe that the revived community policing strategy is working as neighborhood after neighborhood reports safer homes and safer streets.

This brief historical overview of American community policing offers some significant implications and parallels for community policing on the college campus. Just as our country has experienced phenomenal changes in two centuries, so has the college campus. As discussed in Chapter 1, the campus has been in constant transition both responding to societal changes and, in effect, contributing to the educational, economic, and social evolution of the nation. Much like the young developing nation, the college campus was typically tranquil with little serious crime and violence. Essentially, the college campus remained a sanctuary apart from the real world of crime throughout the nineteenth century and the first half of the twentieth century. During the early 1800s, a few isolated student riots, disruptions, and brawls were reported on several American college campuses. Essentially campus crime was of no significance in those early years of American higher education.

A century later the picture changed significantly across the country and on many college campuses. Several major factors came together just prior to and during the 1960s which transformed higher education from its existence in colonial times to the multi-billion dollar industry it is today. These factors included increased enrollments, increased endowments, the Vietnam War, the Civil Rights movement, the popularity of recreational drug use, a social revolution, and program adaptations for nontraditional students. Perhaps the single most influential impact on higher education was federal funding. Such legislation as the National

Defense Education Act of 1958, and the Higher Education Act of 1965 pumped billions of dollars into higher education and resulted in the proliferation of more and larger colleges and universities.

These tremendous impacts on American higher education also caused a dramatic environmental change to the campus, a different social atmosphere. Political and cultural issues became the rallying points for many students. As in the nineteenth century, the 1960s reflect parallels with the campus climate and that of American society. Across the country civil rights demonstrations brought protestors into direct confrontations with police. The frustrations of African-Americans finally exploded into violent disorders in 1964. Student activism was at its height during this period and resulted in clashes with university administrators, local police, and campus security personnel. This social unrest soon dissipated and as campuses continued to expand and enrollments increased, society's ills continued to affect campus communities. Crime came to campus.

Today, crime on campus has become a nationally recognized issue on the agenda of virtually every local, state, and federal politician. Parents and students are demanding better security measures and safer campuses. Faculty at some institutions have urged administrators to enhance campus security and to get tough on criminals—especially student criminals. University administrators are now seeking solutions to campus crime problems. They recognize the importance of creating a safe campus.

## WHAT IS COMMUNITY POLICING?

Community-oriented policing has been defined as a philosophy characterized as a proactive, decentralized approach, designed to reduce crime, disorder, and by extension, fear of crime, by intensively involving the same officers in the same community on a long-term basis, so that residents will develop trust to cooperate with police by providing information and assistance to achieve desired goals.[6] Community policing, whether on campus or in the city, is not only a philosophy in an operational sense, but also a managerial philosophy which emphasizes empowerment. By empowering the officers, supervisors provide them with the authority to use their knowledge, skills, abilities, and values to identify community problems and work collaboratively toward their solution.[7]

The foundations of a successful community policing strategy are the close, mutually beneficial ties between police and community members. Community policing consists of two complementary core components—community partnership and problem solving. To develop partnership, police must develop positive relationships with the community, they must involve the community in the quest for better crime control and prevention, and they must pool their resources with those of the community to address the most urgent concerns of community members. Problem solving is the process through which the specific concerns of communities are identified and through which the most appropriate remedies to abate these problems are found.[8]

Community policing involves the following ten principles:[9]

1. Community policing is both a philosophy and an organizational strategy.
2. Community policing's organizational strategy first demands that everyone in the department, including both civilian and sworn personnel, must investigate new ways to translate the philosophy into practice.
3. To implement true community policing, police departments must also create and develop a new breed of line officer, the Community Policing Officer (CPO).
4. The Community Policing Officer's broad role demands continuous, sustained contact with law-abiding people in the community.
5. Community policing implies a new contract between the police and the citizens it serves, one that offers the hope of overcoming widespread apathy, at the same time it restrains any impulse to vigilantism.
6. Community policing adds a vital proactive element to the traditional reactive role of the police, resulting in full spectrum police service.
7. Community policing stresses exploring new ways to protect and enhance the lives of those who are most vulnerable—juveniles, the elderly, minorities, the poor, the disabled, the homeless.
8. Community policing promotes the judicious use of technology.
9. Community policing must be a full integrated approach that involves everyone in the department, with the CPO's as specialists in bridging the gap between the police and the people they serve.
10. Community policing provides decentralized, personalized police service to the community.

While the above principles outline the characteristics of community policing, there is no single set of strategies that fully captures the essence of community policing. It clearly involves the refocusing of police priorities in such a way so as to emphasize the importance of the campus police and community relationship in effectively addressing pressing crime and security problems while at the same time de-emphasizing the relative unimportance of more traditional police measurement indices.[10]

The university environment should provide an ideal climate for implementing community policing principles.

## IMPLEMENTING COMMUNITY POLICING: ONE UNIVERSITY'S EXPERIENCE

The University of South Florida (USF) Police Department initiated its community policing efforts in 1992. Incorporating community policing into a university law enforcement agency doesn't happen overnight. When implementing community policing the University of South Florida Police Department took the approach that it is a "philosophy" that incorporates the concepts, strategies, and programs of the community policing into all sections within the agency rather than a "program" for which only a few officers are responsible.

The USF Police Department looked at community policing not only as a philosophy in an operational sense, but as a managerial philosophy that emphasizes empowerment. By empowering the officers, supervisors provide them with the authority to use their knowledge, skills, abilities and values to identify problems and work toward their solutions. This empowerment reflects the trust that police leaders have in the officers' abilities to make appropriate decisions. The development of a successful community policing philosophy requires that three basic steps be taken to establish a base on which to build. These include developing a mission statement, surveying the public, and surveying the police officers in the agency.

To set the ground work for implementing a community policing philosophy, the University Police established a clear statement of its mission and philosophy. That mission statement reflected the intent both to continue traditional police responsibilities and to create a philosophy of community responsiveness and cooperative problem solving. In developing a mission statement, a committee that included representatives from each division within the agency was formed, including sworn and civilian employees.

In 1992, the University Police conducted surveys of our students, faculty, and staff to determine if the agency's goals were consistent with the needs and expectations of the community. The survey was used to measure the department's relationship with the community, based upon the public perception.

The survey also revealed the services that the public wanted to see performed by their police department. It additionally provided a useful measure of trends and changing directions of opinions. Finally, the survey was useful in that it provided positive and negative feedback on the public's impression of law enforcement responsiveness.

In order to determine the motivational level of officers, the department surveyed members to determine the level of job satisfaction and/or dissatisfaction among police officers. The results of the survey of the officers helped the agency in determining the level of motivation of the officers and the extent of their knowledge of the community and commitment to community policing.

**Implementation**

Management encouraged collaboration within the ranks and the use of task forces to deal with specific problems. Managers encouraged all officers to use their knowledge, skills, and values to identify problems and work toward solutions. The line officers also began participating in agency decision making. This not only made certain that they felt consulted but it also helped to "get the cards out on the table" so there was a more open forum for competing viewpoints. This was accomplished in ways such as developing a quality management committee consisting of officers of varying ranks and positions, which reviews issues that affect the entire agency, and subject matter experts who provide input on proposed policies and procedures based upon their expertise and/or interest.

The selection process was the starting point for identifying prospective officers who would be successful in community policing. Several characteristics were identified as important to the community policing philosophy. These characteristics included:

An officer who is interested in the problems of crime and disorder.

An officer who derives job satisfaction from seeing the benefits of his or her labor and receives positive feedback from the job.

An officer who can adapt to a community/neighborhood perspective of law enforcement.

An officer who is self-confident and challenges conventional wisdom.

An officer who is creative and resourceful in the job.

An officer who is objective in making decisions and makes those decisions based on collected data.

An officer who has a broad perspective based on prior work experience, education, and an understanding of diverse cultures.

The characteristics and concepts of community policing were incorporated in departmental job descriptions. Next, evaluative standards were modified accordingly for the employees in the agency.

The department wanted to involve patrol officers directly in community-oriented policing (COP) efforts. One way this was accomplished was by having each officer personally select a one-year project that would accomplish one of two things: reduce crime on campus or improve the quality of life within the University community. Outstanding results were accomplished by officers with this approach.

Under community policing, all aspects of officer training were reviewed. Upon graduation from the police academy, and throughout the officer's career, USF continued to stress the proper role of the police in the community. This has helped develop skills in areas such as leadership, community complexities and expectations, and problem-solving procedures. A major emphasis of the training has been in the area of cross-cultural communication, which is critical in a diverse university community. Another focus of our training has been in the area of problem solving. As a fundamental strategy, community policing efforts encourage officers to analyze problems within the community.

Reinforcing the commitment to community policing has best been accomplished by rewarding officers who take actions that exemplify the philosophy. Once again, this "right conduct" must fall within the general guidelines of reducing crime on the campus or improving the quality of life within the university community.

Rewards have been a powerful motivator for employees. Several means of rewarding officer conduct have been used. These include performance evaluations, meritorious awards, an officer of the year award, various commendations, and providing opportunities to attend special training courses.

The success of a community policing program is based on the efforts of the individual officer. It also involves broad measures of success such as the quality of life in neighborhoods, reduction of citizen fear, increased public order, and community satisfaction with police services.

Traditionally, quantitative measurements of an officer's activity, such as number of reports written, number of arrests made, number of calls answered, or number of traffic tickets issued, have been used as a means of gauging an officer's performance. These measures are lacking when attempting to evaluate the delivery of police services, community satisfaction and other key elements of community policing.

Qualitative measures of an officer's performance, such as communication skills, quality of decisions, or how an officer relates to the public, are difficult to substantiate. Nevertheless, these measures can provide a clear indication of an officer's community policing orientation. There are several methods used to provide nontraditional qualitative measurements of progress. One involves periodically conducting a public survey. This will give the agency an opportunity to determine if the community's opinion of them has changed as the community policing philosophy has developed. Conducting a public survey every three or four years will ensure that the department will be kept up to date on changes in public perception and help to focus police/community initiatives.

The transformation to a philosophy of community policing is not accomplished by issuing a directive or statement of intent. Instead, it is accomplished by a deliberate, planned, long-term effort dedicated to changing attitudes and involving the community in solving the problems of crime within the community.

## READINESS AND ASSESSMENT

The implementation of a community policing program on campus is a complicated and multifaceted process that, in essence, requires planning and managing change. Community policing cannot be established through a mere modification of existing policy; profound changes must occur on every level and in every area of the police/security organization. Every employee in the organization must be at the appropriate readiness level. This means that preliminary orientation must ready the officers and other staff members. They should understand the philosophy, mission, goals, objectives, and practical strategies for effectively implementing community policing on campus. The mission statement must reflect the intent both to continue certain aspects of traditional responsibilities and to create a philosophy of community responsiveness and cooperative problem solving.

Employees should then be ready to translate the philosophy, mission, and goals into day-to-day activities. They are on the cutting edge of this change process and, thus, understand and embrace the principles of community policing. They must be empowered to assist students and faculty members in solving problems and creating a positive campus climate.

From the very beginning and throughout the implementation of community policing on campus, ongoing assessment activities should be in place. Assessment helps give the organization a clear sense of direction and allows campus police/security officials to focus efforts on the most efficient and productive practices. Therefore, assessment is indispensable in determining which elements of community policing should be maintained, altered, or eliminated and offers key decision makers, such as college presidents, a way to gauge the impact and cost-effectiveness of community policing efforts.

Giving campus community members a way to measure the success of community policing efforts is critical to maintaining strong ties, ensuring continued participation, and documenting the progress made. Officers themselves will benefit from ongoing evaluation which will reveal their effectiveness. Key student groups include the student government association, Greek organizations, campus housing associations, and minority groups. Methods which may be used to solicit feedback include surveys, group meetings, one-to-one contacts, student/faculty customer contact forms, and analysis of community participation. Of course, the bottom line for evaluating a community policing effort is a reduction in crime and problem-solving successes.

## STRATEGIES FOR EFFECTIVENESS

### Community Policing and Campus Housing

On campuses where students and staff are housed, whether in residence halls, apartments, fraternity houses, or other dwellings most criminal incidents occur there just as most crimes in other communities are committed in and around residential areas. It is therefore important that campus police/security officials conduct a comprehensive crime analysis or assessment of the "when," "where," and "who" of criminal incidents. A case in point is Jacksonville State University (JSU) located Jacksonville, Alabama. JSU is a state institution with an enrollment of approximately 8,000 students with an on-campus population of about 2,000. During most of the 1980s, the JSU Police Department (JSUPD) operated, by and large, in the traditional way—routine vehicular patrol. These patrols were random and covered a two-mile radius to include academic buildings, athletic facilities, dormitories, and campus-owned apartments on the fringes of the campus property. During the late 1980s, the JSUPD began to conduct crime analyses. The assessment findings revealed that 63 percent of all criminal incidents occurred in and/or around residential facilities—primarily residence halls (see Figure 6.1). In fact this analysis of crime statistics indicated that more than 90 percent of crimes of violence were committed in and/or around residence halls. Also revealed was the fact that most crimes occurred at nighttime (see Figure 6.2). This was somewhat disturbing to JSUPD administrators since the patrol efforts had been generally evenly distributed to all parts of the campus. It was obvious that existing policing methods were not effective, especially since the campus crime rate had steadily risen over the previous four years. Consequently, JSUPD officials determined to turn the tide by implementing a community-oriented policing approach.

It is incumbent on campus public safety leaders to provide the education, training, and direction for creating a safe campus. Community policing, when appropriately applied, is the best approach for solving the crime problems and reducing the risks. Traditional policing with its ineffective "preventive patrol" is not working either in the community or on campus. Riding around aimlessly in patrol cars serves little real crime prevention purpose. It is time to refocus goals and reorient our personnel toward community-based, citizen involved crime prevention strategies.

Residential facilities have unique needs which call for programming focused on resident students. Typically, most colleges and universities have relied on dormitories or residence halls for housing students. These facilities house large numbers of students under one roof and have characteristics similar to high-rise apartment complexes. Perhaps the primary difference is the residents themselves. In a typical college dormitory residents are between the ages of seventeen and twenty-four with an educational level higher than the national average and who reside there with a common purpose—to get a degree. These mostly single young multicultural adults have a propensity to indulge in alcohol to excess and enjoy late-night social activities. In many cases, they share a small room with one or two other students. Such close living conditions create a variety of related problems such as noise complaints, drunkenness, disputes, a high rate of thefts, and racial tensions.

Consequently, crime prevention programming for campus housing should be an essential component of the community policing effort. By establishing a partnership between the campus police department and housing officials, a better understanding of problems and issues can be

**Figure 6.1**

## UNIVERSITY POLICE DEPARTMENT
## CRIMES BY LOCATION 1990-1991

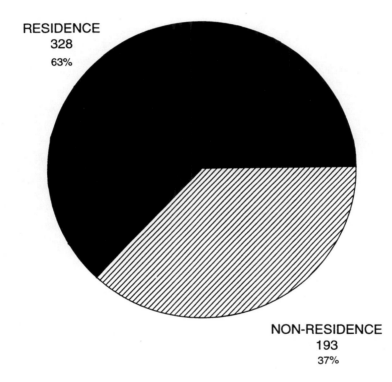

RESIDENCE
328
63%

NON-RESIDENCE
193
37%

developed. Further, problem-solving strategies will be based on creative ideas from students, resident assistants, dormitory directors, apartment managers, programming coordinators, and other housing staff. Coupled with recommendations and procedures emanating from police/security officers, these ideas will result in practical applications for making resident halls and apartments more safe and secure. While programming is only one aspect of the comprehensive community policing effort, it is important in that it allows police/security officers opportunities to work closely with housing officials in developing meaningful presentations, to

**Figure 6.2**

## UNIVERSITY POLICE DEPARTMENT
## CRIMES BY TIME 1990-1991

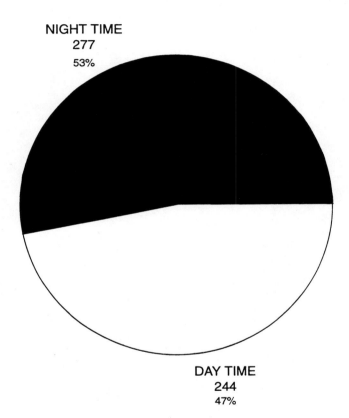

NIGHT TIME
277
53%

DAY TIME
244
47%

make personal contacts with students, to share information, and to participate in student activities in and around residential facilities. Programming may include, but not be limited to, crime prevention videos and presentations by police security officers police ride-along activities for students, joint athletic activities sponsored by the campus police/security department, awards for crime-free dormitories, crime prevention week activities, alcohol/drug awareness presentations, and self-defense classes.

**Police/Security Presence—Breaking Down Barriers**

Making community policing work with campus residential facilities will require almost a total abandonment of the traditional patrol approach with all its barriers. The effect of officers patrolling around campus in automobiles is of little significance in deterring crime. Routine patrol has proven to be of almost no proven value on crime prevention as evidenced by the famous Kansas City Patrol Experiment.[11] Shoemaker and Gerlach succinctly put it in perspective:

> Many recent articles and publications have been devoted to the incidence of crime on campus and its impact. Many law enforcement administrators view the annual 10%–15% increase in crime as a reflection of a nationwide trend. Others view the trend as an indictment of "traditional" forms of law enforcement which rely on high performance vehicles; computers in cars, and on every desk; expensive truncated radios; paramilitary weapons and tactical teams; and more police driving endlessly on our streets. This is the wrong plan for today, and no matter how many more toys, bells and whistles we buy, we'll continue to loose ground.[12]

A successful campus community oriented policing program will take police/security officers out of their patrol vehicles more often and have them "personalize" their crime prevention and public relations efforts with students, staff, and visitors. Those who reside in campus residential facilities such as dormitories are the campus police/security officers' citizens and customers. The on-site presence of patrol officers and the opportunity for one-on-one contacts in and around residential facilities develops special relationships for solving crime and security problems.

There are certainly other activities which campus public safety departments can initiate that will increase a "presence" in residential facilities. Some university police/security agencies utilize student security monitors in and around residence halls. These extra eyes and ears provide heightened security and ease students' anxieties about intruders. Under a partnership approach housing staffs may also use student workers as desk assistants, monitors, and security guards. These students should have a prescribed procedure for reporting any incidents to the campus public safety office.

The methods of patrol in and around residence halls should include foot patrols, bicycle patrols, vehicle patrols, and stationary assignments in special areas. A combination of these is recommended. The level and type of patrol for residential facilities depends on several factors. One is the frequency of crime and security violations. For example, if a particular residence hall has experienced several incidents of trespassing by outside intruders, a stationary "in-dorm" walking patrol officer may be assigned until these incidents diminish. Also, increased vehicle, bicycle, and walking patrols may be indicated during these periods of crime problems.

Another factor in determining the level and type of patrol for residential facilities is the kind of facility itself. On-campus apartments for example, may not be as conducive to inside walk-through patrols but may call for bicycle patrols and "walk-arounds."

The time of day and time of year may also influence the level and type of patrol. Nighttime may demand greater emphasis than daytime on some campuses. The summer months on some campus may find significantly lower occupancy rates and, consequently, lower crime rates.

Whatever patrol technique used to enhance police/security presence, a major purpose remains to be positive public relations and partnership development between police/security officers and the residents. This should always be major focus. This is not a separate issue but a basis component of effective campus community policing.

**Other Strategies**

While this discussion is not intended to be an exhaustive one, a few other strategies are recommended to enhance the community policing efforts for campus residential facilities. A novel program used on some campuses (perhaps taken from municipal community policing) is "Adopt-A-Cop." Under this concept, one or two campus police/security officers are "adopted" by a residence hall or apartment. This partnership approach benefits both the housing department and the public safety department by bringing together both staffs to work toward a common goal—crime prevention. It is of particular advantage to the police/security officials in that it places the officers "inside" the community to assist in residents solving their own problems. Certainly, officers must be carefully selected and oriented before being assigned to these strategic activities.

A more commonly used program is the female security escort service. While this is normally used campus-wide, it is of particular significance to the resident students. These extend the service mission of the campus police/security department directly to students in a meaningful way while instilling a sense of safety among all students. Some universities use residence halls as "home base" for these security escorts, further enhancing the "presence" factor.

There are certainly a host of other strategies for creating safer campus housing via the community policing approach. These include but are not limited to the following:

1. Collaborative development of guidelines for alcohol consumption policy.
2. Creative approaches to access control measures.
3. Special student-police developed security strategies for social events held in residence halls.
4. Programming for reducing the possession and threat of firearms.
5. A housing staff, student, and police/security assessment study to determine the vulnerability of residence halls and apartments along with effective recommendations for improvements.
6. A "ride-along" program for students to ride with camp police to gain an understanding and appreciation of their role and duties.

## COMMUNITY POLICING ON CAMPUS: A COMMUNITY PARTNERSHIP

Establishing and maintaining mutual trust is an essential component of community policing. In essence, this creates a community partnership. Campus police should recognize the need for cooperation with all segments of the community. In turn, community members must accept their shared responsibility in working with the police to create safe streets and communities. Community partnership means adopting a policing perspective that exceeds the traditional law enforcement emphasis. This broadened outlook recognizes the value of activities that contributes to the peace and safety of the campus community. To build a genuine trust for this community partnership, campus police/security officers must gain the respect and support of students, faculty, and staff. To do this requires a variety of approaches and strategies. These must be developed in a problem-solving or problem-oriented approach which should involve community members and campus police. When campus residents or police recognize conditions which lend themselves to criminal activity or unsafe circumstances, the joint problem solving strategy should be employed to reduce existing risks and remove, if possible, the unsafe conditions. The concept of community policing puts new emphasis on tackling the underlying causes of crime by addressing problems at the grassroots level.

Effective community partnership and problem solving will require the mastery of new responsibilities and the adoption of a more flexible style of management. Community policing emphasizes the value of the patrol function and the patrol officer as an individual. Under the traditional policing approach patrol officers are generally relegated to a low status with little input into policing and strategy development. Essentially, before launching a genuine community policing program on campus, police and security officials must understand and initiate an organizational change that will replace traditional, para-military model with a more collegial, community-based one. Within the campus environment, public safety administrators must empower officers with more decision-making responsibilities in solving campus crime problems. They must also understand the importance of a partnership with campus community constituents. This is a prerequisite for any successful community policing effort on campus.

## SUMMARY

Community policing on campus has promise for meeting the unique public safety needs of the academic environment. If properly implemented, this community/student-based approach to crime prevention will assist campus police/security officials in their efforts to enhance the quality of life for the institution. This can best be accomplished when the philosophy and mission of community policing is understood and embraced at all levels within the assiduous leadership and clearly articulated support from top administrative officials.

During financially austere times for American higher education, it should be noted that most campus community policing efforts require minimal outlay in terms of personnel, equipment, and facilities. Indications are that these cost-effective programs have already resulted in reduced crime rates as well as improved community relations between campus police and students and faculty. Furthermore, these successful efforts have provided opportunities for campus police organizations to redefine their role toward more customer service and less strict law enforcement. This may well be worth the efforts or organization change that comes with community policing. This will require visionary leadership if organizational change is to remain institutionalized.

Finally, while community policing on campus holds obvious advantages for the campus community, it has no better application than for student housing. Here, students, staff and police/security officers can work together to create a safe and pleasant living environment. While this approach requires a partnership between housing and police, it is the primary responsibility of the campus police/security officials to provide the leadership necessary to initiate efforts and make them work. As with exemplary municipal models for community policing, campus police and security officers assigned to housing areas will need to develop a new mind set to replace the traditional police patrol mentality. All of these efforts will require time, patience, and determination. In the end, the campus should be a safer place to live, work, and learn.

## ENDNOTES

1. Robert P. Johnson, "Implementing Community Policing In A University Environment," *Campus Law Enforcement Journal,* Vol. 24, No. 3, May/June 1994, pp. 17 and 35.
2. Chris Braiden, "Enriching Traditional Police Roles." *Police Management: Issues and Perspectives,* (Washington, D.C.: Police Executive Research Forum, 1992), p. 108.
3. Jerome H. Skolnick, "The Police and the Urban Ghetto," *The Ambivalent Force: Perspectives on Police,* eds. Arthur Niederhoffer and Abraham S. Blumberg, 2d. ed. (Hindsdale, IL: Dryden, 1976), p. 222.
4. Jeffrey Patterson, "Community Policing: Learning the Lessons of History." *FBI Law Enforcement Bulletin,* Vol. 64, No. 11, November 1995, pp. 7 and 8.
5. Ibid, p. 8.
6. Robert C. Trojanowicz, B. Benson and Susan Trojanowicz, *Community Policing: University Input Into Campus Police Policy-Making.* East Lansing, Michigan: National Neighborhood Foot Patrol Center, Michigan State University, School of Criminal Justice, 1988.
7. Johnson, p. 17.
8. Bureau of Justice, *Understanding Community Policing: A Framework for Action,* A monograph, Washington, D.C., 1994, p. 13.
9. Virginia Department of Criminal Justice Services. *Supervisors In Community Policing,* 1994, (1.2 ed).
10. Paul Lang, "Community Policing: A Case for Campus Police." *Community Policing On Campus,* A monograph. (Hartford, Connecticut: International Association of Campus Law Enforcement Administrators, 1995), p. 6.
11. Robert F. Johnson, "Implementing Community Policing: One University's Experience," *Community Policing On Campus,* A monograph (Hartford, Connecticut: International Association of Campus Law Enforcement Administrators, 1995), p. 37–44.
12. Charles R. Swanson, Leonard Territo, and Robert W. Taylor, *Police Adminis-*

*tration,* 2nd Edition, (New York: MacMillan Publishing Company, 1988), p. 521–522.

13. Eric W. Shoemaker and Bill Gerlach, "Matching Perceptions and Reality: Community Oriented Policing", Campus Law Enforcement Journal, Vol. 25 No. 2, March/April 1995, p. 18.

# Chapter 7

# SECURE CAMPUS HOUSING

## INTRODUCTION

A critical component of creating a safe campus is secure campus housing. For most institutions of higher education, students live on or in close proximity to the campus. It is their place of residence where students spend most of their out-of-class experiences. Residence halls, the traditional mode of student housing, continues to provide a "home away from home" for many college students. A growing trend toward on-and-off-campus apartments provide alternative housing arrangements for some students. Research studies clearly indicate that campus residential living creates a social-psychological environment for students that is qualitatively different from those who live at home or elsewhere off campus and commute to college. It is evident that living on campus will maximize opportunities for social, cultural and extracurricular involvement.[1] While campus living is intended to foster student learning through well-planned, safe, integrated, and coherent educational experiences, crime and threats to personal tranquility can diminish the anticipated outcomes and impacts. Most higher education housing professionals realize that many and perhaps most of the incidents of victimization occurring on their campuses occur in their residence halls, primarily because that is where most students on a residential campus are at night and on weekends and it is where alcohol is most often consumed.[2] Apartments, fraternity and sorority houses, and other forms of residence are no exception to this premise. Students dwelling on campus and in nearby housing units may face higher risks of becoming victims of property crimes than the national average. This is due, in part, to the fact that dormitory and apartment living arrangements coupled with student lifestyles would readily lend themselves to more burglary and theft than society at large.[3]

College and university officials should take a close look at the effectiveness of safety and security measures as they relate to residential facilities.

Housing professionals should ensure that a security component be a top priority among their goals and objective for residence life. Students, too, should embrace their role and share responsibility in making their "home away from home" a safe and tranquil place to live, learn, and play.

## RESIDENCE LIFE ON AND AROUND CAMPUS

Today's campus housing has deep roots in American higher education. Residential facilities, originally referred to as dormitories, were rooted in the English universities on which American higher education was modeled. In the early colonial colleges, dormitories became an essential aspect of what was known as the collegiate way of life. In these early years, faculty members were directly involved in out-of-class activities, especially on-campus living. For a period following the Civil War, a new breed of higher education leaders determined that residential living should be separate from and unrelated to the intellectual life of the classroom and laboratory.[4]

The nineteenth century brought significant changes to housing management. As faculty members were expected to increase their service and research activities, they had less time to devote to students' out-of-class activities. Consequently, the role of the dean of students emerged as the official responsible for residence life to include student behavior.[5]

During the mid-twentieth century interests and values changed, student affairs positions were created to attend to the aspects of student life no longer guided by faculty members. At the same time students of more diverse backgrounds, needs, and interests were entering higher education, and enrollments soared. The student activism and national upheaval of the tumultuous 1960s resulted in dramatic changes for residence halls. Students' demand for freedom from control and supervision resulted in the establishment of coeducational halls, visitation with fewer restrictions, elimination of curfews, and more lax rules for alcohol in rooms. A new legalistic definition of the student-institution (akin to landlord-tenant) relationship replaced the long-standing doctrine of *in loco parentis*. Further, the new student development perspective which emphasized the holistic approach had a profound impact on the roles and functions of residence life. Assuming such roles as educators, counselors, and managers, residence life staff members responded to an increasingly diverse student culture, to problems of alcohol and drug abuse, and to student misconduct.[6] This student development movement has guided housing professionals through the nineties. While trends and innovative programs continue to create new approaches and improved methods, today's residence life officials are generally committed to creating an environment which enhances the quality of life of student as they pursue social, personal, physical, psychological, and academic goals.

Residence halls or dormitories remain the predominate type of campus housing. While architectural designs and accommodations vary, the typical residence hall houses from several dozen student residents to several hundred. They are likely to be multistory buildings with entry to rooms on interior hallways. There are usually several entrances and exits to the buildings and, unfortunately, many older residence halls have no effective security hardware designed to keep out intruders. Residence halls usually have entryway lobbies, special meeting rooms, TV rooms, and laundry rooms. Some have centralized kitchens and older halls still utilize community restrooms and showers designed for same-gender usage. Many residence halls constructed since the 1970s feature private restrooms with each room. Residence halls may house same-gender only or may be coed. Cornell University may be the first institution to allow "program houses" which, in essence, designate special cultural preference for living in residence halls. There, three residence halls are each designated as African-American, Latino, or American Indian culture. Any student may choose to reside in these halls.[7]

The trend is toward making residence halls as much like apartments as possible. Through either renovation of older, historically significant halls or construction of new buildings, college officials are including private baths, wiring for cable and computers and kitchens.[8]

These unique characteristics create close living conditions for young single adults who are often away from home for the first time. Add to this mix a wide disparity of social and cultural diversity. In a research study which looked at victimization in residence halls, the author presents the central issue:

> The ultimate question of concern involves how higher education can assist students of many races, nations, religions, cultures, lifestyles, etc., in learning to live, learn, and work together in harmony with a recognition of their similarities and with an appreciation for their many differences.[9]

Thus residence hall living presents special issues and problems for higher education officials, and in particular housing officials, in their efforts to create a safe and tranquil environment. The challenge may not be only to keep a safe fortress free from outside intruders but rather to maintain peace and promote harmony within the residence hall among a diverse student residency.

## On-Campus Apartments

On-campus apartments are found on many campuses. These vary widely in their style and arrangements but generally compare to apartments found in the local community. Campus efficiency apartments are popular for college students since they are usually small and affordable. Through expansion moves, some universities purchase existing apartment buildings located on property near the campus and rent or lease the apartment units to students. This category of housing will be discussed in the next section.

Apartment living differs in significant ways from life in a residence hall. Apartment units are usually designed to afford a greater degree of privacy and independence. Typically, there is no interior common hallway. Further, apartment units have kitchen facilities, private baths, and living rooms, all of which do not allow for the camaraderie and social interaction found in such areas in residence halls.

Apartment buildings are also managed differently than residence halls. Apartment managers are not in direct contact with residents as are hall directors and student resident assistants. Because of this and the architectural design differences, students experience less scrutiny and more independence from campus authority. Also, some campus rules and regulations, such as alcohol and drug use may be more difficult to monitor and enforce when students live in apartments. Nontraditional students, i.e., married students, older students, etc., are sometimes assigned to campus apartments.

Security for on-campus apartments will require special approaches and, in fact, shift the burden of responsibility more heavily on students themselves. On some campuses, apartments are located away from other residential facilities and often away from the main campus. This may require special patrol efforts by police/security officers. Lack of access control to apartment buildings may also prevent security problems.

## On-Campus Houses

Some college and universities provide houses on their campus. Houses may include traditional homes for faculty, staff, and students or they may be houses used by Greek organizations such as found on a traditional fraternity row. Generally, houses are located in separate areas of the campus from residence halls. They may be managed under the auspices of the campus housing offices or may be found under the business office or auxiliary services division.

Security approaches will likely differ from those of residence halls. The responsibility for security, behavior, and regulations will rest heavily on the occupants or tenants. Programming by housing staff or police personnel would not be found as frequent as it might be conducted in residence halls. Security measures employed and the police response approach would be similar to that found in the local community. This means that little or no emphasis is placed on prevention and that police intervention is in response to calls for service from the residence.

### Off-Campus Housing

For the purposes of this discussion, there are three categories of off-campus housing. One includes housing units, whether houses or apartments, which are owned and operated by the university. The second category is housing not owned by the institution but is located near the campus and which presents special concerns for campus officials. The third is quasi-university related housing — recognized Greek organizations' houses (fraternities and sororities).

Increasingly, university officials are purchasing properties beyond the original boundaries of the campus. In many instances, this property includes houses and/or apartment complexes which the university continues to rent or lease to tenants — usually students. This type of expansion also involves the added responsibility for security and police services just as is provided to other campus residents. A problem often encountered with the purchasing of off-campus housing is the level of physical security left behind by the previous owners, (i.e., door locks, window latches, outside lighting, shrubbery, etc.). These inherited problems can be addressed by campus housing, maintenance, and security officials with favorable outcomes. One example of this arrangement is found at the Stetson University College of Law in Gulfport, Florida. There the college owns some forty houses and thirty-two apartment units on previously-owned property just off the main campus.[10]

The category which is most vexing to some university officials is that of student housing in privately-owned housing units which are nearby or adjacent to the campus. While most institutions do not accept responsibility for student safety in these housing units, others consider this unique circumstance to be a student safety issue worth some extended efforts. Officials at both Marquette University[11] and the University of Florida[12] had demonstrated their concern for off-campus apartment-dwelling students through their special crime prevention programming. These will be discussed in greater detail in a later section in this chapter.

Off-campus fraternity and sorority houses also present unique problems. In addition to town-gown issues of noise, behavior, parking, and litter these social organizations frequently are associated with assaults, rape, drunkenness and other crimes which diminish safety and security for students.

## LEADERSHIP FOR CAMPUS HOUSING

Today's campus residence management requires effective leadership. Whether the housing unit is placed under student affairs, auxiliary services, or some other organizational position, there must be leaders dedicated to creating a safe living environment for all residents. They must understand the significance of campus residence life and its role in the college experience. Campus living, especially in residence halls, affords students that out-of-class experience which will significantly influence their future. Their academic experience will be impacted by the social, cultural, and personal interactions experience in a campus living environment. Housing professionals who appreciate this phenomenon will be better prepared to develop policies and programs which enhance and undergird this valuable experiential opportunity.

Housing leadership should not only understand the dynamics of residential life's influence on student development, they must also be equipped to respond effectively to the rigors of managing the financial and facilities management aspects of the job. Fiscal accountability is an essential competency for successful housing managers. Most institutions expect housing units to eventually make a profit or, as may be asserted, to ensure revenues exceed expenditures. Long-term investments and building depreciation concerns are realities with which housing officials must deal. Consequently, occupancy rates and resident satisfaction are important issues. There may be no single factor which influences these issues more important than perceptions of safety and security. Research studies clearly indicate that campus residential students are particularly susceptible to crime on campus.[13] Therefore, residence life officials should recognize that an important part of their role must be to affect students' beliefs and perceptions pertaining to crime and victimization through safety awareness programming and security measures.

## CAMPUS CRIME AND HOUSING ISSUES

While many of the same problems associated with crime and housing pertain to the campus community generally, the impacts and implications for campus residents are unique. Victimization surveys and campus crime research studies find that campus residents are more likely to be victims of crime than commuter students. Of course, there may be exceptions depending on the circumstances found at institutions, (i.e., local crime rates, access control, parking lot security, rural vs. urban campuses, number of resident students, level of residential security, etc.). Generally, residence halls and other campus residence facilities are locations where crime most likely occurs. The following discussions provide a brief treatment to a few of the categories of crimes in campus housing.

### Violence

Violence in campus housing comes in every form as in society at large. Murder, rape, sexual assault, assault, harassment, fighting, and similar crimes are reported on campuses of all types and sizes across the country. Many of these occur in residence halls. For example, in 1992, Rutgers University officials reported three assaults inside "secure" residence halls in a nine-day period.[14] In 1990, a nonstudent shot to death another nonstudent while visiting in a residence hall on the campus of Jacksonville State University in Alabama. While the victims of residence hall crime vary, residence hall assistants represent the group most likely to be victimized by violence.[15] Of particular concern is the increasing threat of guns and other weapons possessed by students. A survey conducted by the author in 1994 which included 15 colleges and universities in Alabama revealed that 75 percent of campus public safety directors reported firearms possession incidents on their campuses within the past three years.

Rapes, acquaintance rapes, and other forms of sexual assaults in campus residence facilities may be more common than officially reported. One researcher suggested that the most underreported form of violence that occurs in residence halls may be acquaintance rape.[16] This is supported by the Towson State Study which was conducted in 1987. Residence hall directors believed that only 28.8 percent of sexual assaults were actually reported.[17] There is ample evidence to conclude that rape and sexual assault problems do, in fact, exist in campus residence facilities. It is also important to emphasize that few campuses are immune from these threats.

### Alcohol/Drug Problems

Campus safety issues are frequently associated with the use of alcohol and illegal drugs. A recent study conducted by the Harvard School of Public Health revealed that 44 percent of all college students were binge drinkers (five or more drinks in a row one or more times during a two-week period for men, and four or more drinks in a row one or more times during the same period for women).[18] In its report the Harvard study describes the problem:

> Everyone, from the college president down, is susceptible to denial about the extent of the alcohol abuse problem and its impact on the life of the campus. To begin to assess the extent of the problem on a campus, consider a weekend tour, beginning on Thursday night. Take a drive around the campus with the security guards; observe the clubs on its outskirts. Drop in on the health service. On Friday, see how many classes are offered, and how many students attend. Observe the fraternity houses and dorm's late at night; station yourself outside the residence halls and sorority houses Sunday morning and witness the "walk of shame," a phrase students use to describe women returning from a night of unplanned, and often unprotected, sex. Above all, fight the temptation to think of the alcohol abuse you see as merely the problem of "troubled" individuals. When the faces change but the numbers do not, something much more powerful and institutional is happening.[19]

In a similar study in which campus security officials were surveyed regarding alcohol-related problems on campus, 20 percent said there were frequent problems in residence halls related to alcohol. The same survey revealed that 43 percent of security officials felt that alcohol problems were frequent at fraternity events or parties.[20]

The abuse of alcohol is a well-known factor in other crimes in residence facilities to include violence, sexual assaults, assaults, vandalism, and hall crimes. Underage drinking (under age 21) is a common violation among college students. Institutions vary in their approaches to alcohol possession by students. While most have policies which prohibit or restrict alcohol possession, few have developed strategies which have solved the problems associated with alcohol abuse.

Illegal drug use continues to be reported on most college campuses. Residence halls and apartments are perhaps the most likely location for possession and use. Despite their illegal status and potential impacts to residence living, there are indications that drug use may be on the decline. The Harvard study reports that shifts in societal attitudes have played a major role in reducing the use of illegal drugs by college students.[21] This is encouraging but bears cautious monitoring efforts by housing officials and campus law enforcement officers.

### Disruption and Misconduct

Disruption and misconduct are terms as used here to include a wide range of less-than-violent acts, usually perpetrated by student residents themselves. Loud music, vandalism, disorderly behavior, pranks, harassment, panty raids, and routine disputes are among the types of behavior frequently found in college residence halls and other campus residence. While this may appear on the surface to be minor, often disruptive acts and misconduct creates a hostile environment for students. Intimidation and threats may persuade some students to relocate to off-campus housing or leave school altogether.

Residence assistants and hall directors are often the targets of student misconduct—especially harassment. In a study done by Rickarn in 1989, the findings reveal that residence assistants (RA's) who become victims of abuse or harassment may somehow blame themselves for being victimized. They feel loyalty both to their student residents and to their employing institution. In some cases, they are reluctant to even report disruptive or harassing incidents. They may feel pressure due to threats of legal or physical reprisals.[22]

General disorder and reckless behavior can result when sanctions are not consistently used by residence hall and apartment staff. Drunken students walking hallways in a loud and boisterous manner is all too common where such behavior is tolerated. Other conduct which often accompanies this kind of behavior is vandalism, threatening behavior, and harassment targeted toward those of different races, religions, sexual orientations, and cultures.

### Theft

Theft in residence halls is the most common crime found on most campuses. In the 1994 edition of the Federal Bureau of Investigation's *Crime In The United States*, more than 400 colleges and universities submitted numbers for offenses in eight categories that were reported to campus police officials. The category of theft consistently contained the highest reported figures.[23] By and large the majority of campus thefts reported occur in residence facilities. This unique living arrangement provides ideal opportunities for acquaintances and fellow residence to conveniently "lift" items and money from nearby rooms and common areas of unsuspecting residents. Students often unwittingly become easy targets due to their sense of invulnerability and preoccupation with social activities. Unlocked doors, unsecured personal property, and carelessness contribute to the high rate of thefts in many residence facilities.

## STRATEGIES FOR CREATING SAFE RESIDENCES ON CAMPUS

Prior to the development of policies and specific strategies aimed at creating safe campus residence facilities, university officials to include those responsible for housing must first recognize the real problems and issues. They must understand the significant threats to students' safety and grasp the reality of students' perceptions of campus crime and other intimidating misconduct. Second, a "zero tolerance" philosophy toward any form of violence and intrusive behavior must be embraced by all campus administrators, faculty, and staff. Third, officials at all levels must demonstrate their commitment to the values of integrity, fairness, and justice through effective policies, programs, and processes. And fourth, meaningful strategies aimed at enhanced residential security should be developed through thorough assessment processes, long-range planning, and broad-based participation. Institutions of higher education can no longer tolerate escalating crime on their campuses and the victimization of their students. In her book entitled *Violent Crimes and Other Forms of Victimization In Residence Halls,* Carolyn J. Palmers states:

> Clearly, victimization of students must be listed as a priority warranting our continual attention. However, this attention must be provided not only by housing officers, counselors, disciplinary officers, campus police and others who deal most directly with the problem on a day-to-day basis, but by institutional leaders at the very top of the administrative hierarchy.[24]

### Policies, Procedures, and Regulations

College and university residence life and housing officials should formulate and periodically review the policies, procedures, and regulations as they relate to housing security and safety. Policies should include the institutions philosophy and position on the top priority of security and good behavior in residential facilities. These policies along with sanctions may be found in special housing policy books and/or in the university's student handbook. Policies should be written in clear and concise terminology. Policies generally include statements of expected behavior and usually enumerate specific rules and regulations which are prohibited. They typically parallel similar policies and regulations found in university student handbooks.

Procedures for the enforcement and adjudication of policies should also be spelled out. Residence life departments may utilize their own judicial procedures for dealing with specific housing violations. These may be "stand alone" processes or they may be conducted in conjunction with or preceding a separate university judicial process for a violation of a broader university student conduct code. The following is a sample of a typical housing judicial proceeding process:

### Access Control

Institutions with resident students should assess the feasibility and desirability of having and enforcing rules restricting access to student housing. Access control has proven to be a critical issue in serious criminal incidents in campus residential facilities. One of the most publicized incidents occurred in 1986 on the campus of Lehigh University in Pennsylvania. Jeanne Cleary was brutally raped and murdered in a campus resident hall. The perpetrator gained entrance through an unsecured resident hall. As a result of that incident and the efforts of her parents, Howard and Constance Cleary, increased attention through legislation has been given to enhancing campus residence security. With this heightened awareness of campus crime and, specifically, residence hall incidents, the perceived threat of unauthorized entry into institutional residence facilities has become a significant concern for campus officials. Campus residence facilities (residence halls, apartments, fraternity and sorority houses, etc.) often represent the most potential crime targets at a college or university.

Recent court decisions have reaffirmed the responsibility of colleges and universities to provide an adequate level of safety and security on campus. Since providing student housing is essentially a proprietary function, an institution of higher education may find itself in a similar position to a landlord with respect to its duty to exercise due care for its

**Figure 7.1**

## JUDICIAL PROCEEDING

**Initiating procedure:**
There are two ways in which charges may be filed and a case may be heard before the Department of Student Housing and Residence Life Judicial bodies.
1. An incident report may be filed by; any Housing Employee, University Police Officer, or Security Guard
2. Any resident may report an alleged violation of University policy, or if that individual feels that his or her rights have been violated by another member of the residence hall community. Such a report must be filed with the Residence Hall Director, who will investigate the allegations and take appropriate action.

**Notice:**
A resident charged with an alleged violation of University policy shall be given written notice within a reasonable amount of time. This notice shall include: the date, time and place of the hearing. A copy of the Incident Report may be obtained at the Department of Student Housing and Residence Life.

**Hearing**
If a resident is charged with a violation of policy there are two recourses for hearing:
1. The Residence Hall Director
2. The Behavior Standards Board

If the resident charged with a policy violation has not been found guilty of any prior violation in a calendar year, their case may be heard by the Residence Hall Director. The case goes to the Behavior Standards Board if: 1) it is of a serious nature that could best be handled by the Behavioral Standards Board; 2) the resident has been found guilty of a prior violation. 3) If the resident chooses to appear before the Board. The Hearing shall be closed to the public. The accused shall have an opportunity to present a defense either oral or by written statement. The accused may call witnesses to speak in his or her behalf. The accused has the right to have counsel present, but only in an advisory capacity. Formal rules of evidence and procedure shall not be followed. The burden of proof is on the party or entity bringing the charge.

If a Resident scheduled to appear before the BSB wishes to plead guilty to the charges they may contact the Department of Student Housing and Resident Life and set up a time for their case to be sanctioned by the chairperson of the BSB.

If a person scheduled to appear before the Board fails to come to the hearing, the Board will rule on the case.

**Jurisdiction:**
The Department of Student Housing and Residence Life's judicial body hears cases involving Housing policy violation or University policy violations, occurring within or in the immediate area of the Residence Hall.

**Figure 7.1 Continued**

**Current Sanctions:**

| | |
|---|---|
| 1st offense: | $25 fine—MANDATORY |
| | Additional sanctions determined by RHD or BSB. |
| 2nd offense: | $50 fine—MANDATORY |
| | Appropriate Counseling-Optional. |
| | If visitation violation: Suspension of visitation privileges for period determined by the BSB–MANDATORY; Additional sanctions determined by BSB |
| 3rd offense: | $100—MANDATORY |
| | Automatic removal from University Housing—MANDATORY; SUSPENSION FROM THE UNIVERSITY THROUGH THE VICE CHANCELLOR FOR STUDENT AFFAIRS—Optional |
| Additional Sanctions: | Notice sent to Sorority, Fraternity, ROTC, group. |
| | Community Services |
| | Restitution for Damages |
| | University Disciplinary Probation. |

**Suspension of Visitation Privileges.** Visitation privileges can be suspended for first time policy violations as determined by the RHD, and will be suspended for all consecutive policy violations as determined by the BSB. While a resident's visitation privileges are suspended that resident may not check-in guests of the opposite sex nor be checked-in by a resident of the opposite sex. Residents who violate this sanction face possible criminal charges for trespassing.

**Alcohol Policy Violation.** In addition to the above sanctions, all alcohol policy violations will be directed to Assistant Dean of Students. Students found in violation of the Alcohol policy may be required to receive counseling from the Bessie Speed and Wellness Center and will also have notices sent to their parents concerning their policy violation.

**Appeals Procedure:**

Residents wishing to appeal the decision of the BSB must adhere to the following ascending order of appeal:

Board of Trustees
Chancellor
Vice Chancellor for Student Affairs
Director of Student Housing and Residence Life
Behavioral Standards Board
Residence Hall Director

**Figure 7.1. Continued**

Resident wishing to appeal a decision of the BSB needs to submit a written statement listing the reasons for the appeal to the Department of Student Housing and Residence Life. This statement must reach the office within 24 hours of the BSB hearing. Upon receiving the written statement the Director will review the documentation and call an additional hearing or let the decision stand.

tenants (student residents). This duty arises particularly where danger is foreseeable.

In addition to intensive crime awareness programming (as discussed in the next section), effective access control measures may deter would-be perpetrators of criminal acts—both against persons and property. The type and level of residence security access control should be determined by officials at each institution. While some institutions allow student input regarding the kind of restrictions imposed on residence access, officials should use caution when making this critical decision since it will be the institution's officials who may be held liable for negligence claims due to a lack of adequate security. A variety of access control options are available. The following list offers some of these options:[25]

> Lock all exterior doors to student housing buildings, either 24 hours or at designated times such as nighttime. Access would be limited to one or two main entrances where only residents would have keys or other authorized means of access. The removal of outer door handles to some locked doors might also reduce ease of access.
>
> Implement a two-barrier locking system which requires a key or card not only for exterior doors, but also for interior doors and elevators.
>
> Replace first-barrier key locking devices with a push-button, number combination locking system.
>
> Install peep holes on all individual room doors.
>
> Place delayed alarms on all exterior doors, so that if a door is propped a signal sounds both on site and remote to a central security monitoring station.
>
> Install a free telephone line or buzzer outside each housing unit which enables visitors to contact residents in their rooms, reducing the incentive for students to prop exterior doors.
>
> Place proctors/monitors at the entrance of each student housing facility to monitor and restrict access, either on a 24-hour basis or at designated times. These proctors/monitors might have two-way radio communication with campus police and security officers in the event of an intruder.
>
> Ensure that all doors and locks in residential buildings are adequate to prevent unauthorized entry.

Install effective locks, security screens, security bars, and/or other security devices on all windows which would be accessible to intruders.

Install key pads connected to locking devices. A personal identification number (PIN) would be used to gain access.

Install electronic card access control systems.

Electronic access to residence facilities have become more widely used in recent years. There are several configurations and approaches to electronic access. Currently, the three most popular options are: (1) a picture ID that allows students to use a card reader, (2) a plain card with no identifying characteristics, or (3) a semiconductor microchip touch entry device. A combination of these options is often recommended to prevent abuse and easy unauthorized use of a single option. The campus housing office is the logical point for controlling issuance of access codes for residential buildings. The campus police/security office, because of the usual 24-hour operation, should have the capability and authority to issue temporary residence access as well as a method of terminating an access code of a stolen or lost card or compromised code number.[26]

Video surveillance is another method of controlling access. Cameras can be installed in residence hall lobbies, and entrances, in parking lots, in apartment walkways, gateways, and any other logical location which has no expectation to privacy. These cameras should be monitored at a central location on a 24-hour basis.

## Programming

While sound policies and effective access control measures are essential to secure campus housing, they will be of little value without the cooperation and participation of the student residents themselves. Many college students tend to be careless and often preoccupied. They typically have no sense of vulnerability and make prime targets for could-be criminals. Despite strict policies and tight security, students who leave their doors unlocked and ignore security procedures actually contribute to a diminished level of safety and security for their residence.

It is important that housing, security, and student affairs officials develop programs which increase the awareness, knowledge, and sensitivity to safety and security issues in and around campus resident facilities. This effort requires creativity and persistence on the part of institution officials. Students must be made aware of the need for good security. They must be sensitized to the potential of becoming victimized. And, certainly they must understand that creating a safe living environment is a shared responsibility for which they have a vested interest to fulfill.

Ideas for security programming in residence halls are almost limitless. Programs should be tailored to the unique needs of individual campus and, specifically, individual residence facilities. What works for an all-female residence hall on an urban university campus may not be appropriate for a coed apartment building on the campus in a small, rural college. College officials should carefully assess the needs of their residents and the foreseeability of incidents. Money should never be a determining factor when security needs of students are indicated.

The following list offers some programming ideas. This list is certainly not all inclusive, but represents several programs which have proven effective on some campuses.

- Regular floor meetings in residence halls to discuss security issues and develop plans and programs.
- Special crime prevention brochures aimed at residence students' safety.
- Special crime prevention decals or stickers for placement on telephones, bulletin boards, doors, etc. which provide emergency telephone numbers.
- Doorknob hangers are reminders to lock doors and secure rooms and valuables.
- Crime prevention flyers which are widely distributed through campus mail, under individual room doors, on automobile windshields, in restrooms, etc.
- Crime prevention posters located in high traffic areas and which illustrate simple safety/security tips.
- Special personal safety seminars and workshops on such topics as assault, rape awareness, vehicle security, self defense, etc.
- Resident hall and apartment literature, videos, booklets, etc. made available to all campus residence.
- Special security-related presentations at freshmen orientation sessions.
- Community-oriented policing programs for apartments and residence halls such as an "Adopt-A-Cop" program (Discussed in a later chapter).
- Neighborhood watch programs which encourage awareness, monitoring, and reporting of all suspects and suspicious behavior.

- Special emphasis programs such as Operation Identification," bicycle security, female security escort service, emergency telephones, sexual assault/violence counseling, victims advocacy centers, etc.

Perhaps the most effective and enduring programs in residence facilities are those which are developed at least in part, by students themselves. Not only are these often better conceived programs but students may be willing to comply more readily with student-implemented procedures. Student government associations, Greek organizations, and other special interest students groups are good vehicles for developing and promoting safety/security programs for residential facilities. By involving students, campus officials demonstrate a "shared responsibility" approach.

## OFF-CAMPUS HOUSING

Safety and security at off-campus housing facilities has become an important issue for many colleges and universities. For many institutions, off-campus housing is the residence of choice. For others, campus residential facilities simply will not accommodate all students who wish to live on campus. Housing units located off the premises of the main campus property may create special security concerns for university officials. In some off-campus apartments, houses, and fraternity houses security measures are often inadequate. Crime is often a greater threat to students than to those on campus. Perhaps a central question which often arises is: Does the institution have a responsibility to enhance student security at off-campus locations? Generally, most institutions accept no claim to authority or for responsibility for nonuniversity owned premises. This is a policy decision which must be made by each institution. There is evidence, however, that increasingly institutions are becoming proactive in enhancing security for students at off campus locations.

As described earlier, the three categories identified under the term "off-campus housing" include: (1) University-owned housing at off campus locations (away from the main campus), (2) Privately owned housing units off campus, (3) University-recognized fraternity/sorority organizations' houses located off campus. These categories may include various types of housing units such as single family dwellings (houses), apartments, mobile homes, and fraternity/sorority houses. By and large, the scope of this off-campus housing issue is limited to housing within a close proximity to the campus (i.e., adjacent to, within a few blocks, or within a mile radius).

One case study which has received wide attention is the University of Florida in Gainesville. There the University promotes safety near campus through a program in which trained officers inspect off-campus apartments to identify potential danger areas and certify compliance with a set of recommended safety rules.

The Off-Campus Apartment Inspection Program began in 1992 following the murders of five students who lived near the campus in Gainesville. A sliding glass door was installed incorrectly at one of the homicide sites, which prompted university officials to step up their off-campus safety and security policies.

University police officers take a state-level course in environmental design and residence security, after which they are certified to conduct inspections of off-campus apartment buildings. Local city and county police also take the course and help the university officers conduct the inspections. Some of the key safety standards recommended by inspectors include:

- locks on all windows
- a peephole on the front doors
- a minimum length for deadbolt locks to deter tampering
- proper installation of sliding glass doors
- fire extinguishers
- exterior lighting that promotes safety
- well-trimmed shrubs and landscaping

Since university officials recognize that not all students are safety conscious, this program is intended to assist off-campus resident students in being more secure in their residences. Students are appreciative of these efforts. Apartment owners are also receptive.

About 40,000 students attend the University of Florida, but the institution has residence hall space for only about 8,000. Most off-campus students prefer apartment living, especially since there are few rental homes in the area.[27]

## SUMMARY

Secure campus housing is an essential component in creating a safe campus. It is incumbent on housing officials to recognize that the quality of life in residence halls and apartments is, in part, based on the quality of safety and security measures. The uniqueness of residence hall living and its impact on underclassmen is a critical part of the college experience. However, since many first-time college students come to campus with little awareness of their vulnerability, security measures should be in place which transcend their lack of safety consciousness.

Security efforts for campus residential facilities must be designed to protect students from outside intruders as well as from other students. National crime statistics indicate that most crimes are perpetrated by students on other students. For this reason, policies and procedures, access control, and security programs must be developed with a comprehensive approach. Students should share in developing security strategies. An important philosophy which should undergird these strategies should be one of "shared responsibility" by students.

Security for off-campus residences at nearby areas should be a concern for university officials. Whether the institution itself extends its jurisdiction and/or assistance in this regard is a decision for each institution to make. With an increasing number of students living at off-campus residences, officials should be willing to work collaboratively with local proprietors and community officials to enhance safety and security at these near-campus locations.

Crime statistics at many institutions reveal that a major portion of reported criminal incidents occur in and around residence halls and campus apartments. In these cases, it behooves campus officials to give top priority to enhancing housing safety and security measures. This is critical for several reasons. Due to the concept of foreseeability and well-documented court cases involving duty of care and negligence, college administrators face the issue of liability. Also, an increase in crime and violence in campus residences can have a direct negative impact on occupancy rates. And, finally, reports of crime in residence halls, especially crime of violence, will create significant public relations problems for the institution.

## ENDNOTES

1. Charles C. Schroeder, Phyllis Mable, and Associates, *Realizing The Educational Potential of Residence Halls* (San Francisco: Jossey-Bass Publishers, 1994), p. 25.
2. Carolyn J. Palmer, *Violent Crimes and Other Forms of Victimization In Residence*

*Halls* (Asheville, North Carolina: College Administration Publications, Inc., 1993), p. xi.

3. Michael Clay Smith and Richard Fossey, *Crime On Campus: Legal Issues and Campus Administration* (Phoenix, Arizona: American Council On Education, Oryx Press, 1995), p. 16.

4. Ernest L. Boyer, *College: The Undergraduate Experience in America* (New York: Harper Collins, 1987), p. 96.

5. Schroeder and Mable, p. 7.

6. Ibid., p. 8.

7. Christopher Shea, "Cornell 'Program Houses' Satisfy N.Y. Agency", *The Chronicle of Higher Education*, Vol. XVI, No. 44, July 14, 1995, p. A30.

8. Christopher Shea, "Dorms for the '90s", *The Chronicle of Higher Education*, Vol. XVI, No. 44, July 14, 1995, p. A27.

9. Palmer, p. 12.

10. Donald W. Howard, "Off-campus Safety and Security Housing Inspections", *Campus Law Enforcement Journal*, Vol. 24, No. 4, July/August, 1994, p. 29.

11. *Campus Security Report*, "Off-campus Public Safety Office 'Pays Dividends' In Lower Crime," (Port Washington, New York: Rusting Publications, January, 1993), Vol. 5, No. 1, p. 2.

12. Angie Tipton, "Apartment Inspection Program at the University of Florida," *Campus Law Enforcement Journal*, Vol. 22, No. 6, November/December, 1992, p. 32.

13. Tammy J. Lenski, "Students' Perception of Campus Safety and the Effect On Intended Precautionary Behavior," Association of College and University Housing Officers-International, Research and Educational Foundation, Columbia, South, Carolina, May 1992.

14. *Campus Security Report*, "Student Carelessness Tied to Assaults In Locked Residence Hall," Volume 5, Number 1, January 1993, p. 1.

15. Palmer, p. 25.

16. Ibid. 7.

17. "Campus Violence Survey," (unpublished compilation), Office of Student Services, Towson State University, 1987.

18. *Harvard School of Public Health*, Boston, Massachusetts (Funded by the Robert Wood Johnson Foundation), "Binge Drinking On American College Campuses", August 1995, p. 4.

19. Ibid, p. 13.

20. *Center for Alcohol and Other Drug Prevention*, (Bethesda, Maryland: U.S. Department of Education, 1993), "Enforcing the Minimum Age Drinking Law: A Survey of College Administrators and Security Chiefs", p. 5.

21. *Harvard School of Public Health*, p. 12.

22. Gerald Amanda, *Coping With The Disruptive College Student: A Practical Model*, (Asheville, North Carolina: College Administration Publications, Inc., 1994), p. 42.

23. *Crime In The United States, 1994*, (Washington, D.C.: U.S. Department of Justice, Federal Bureau of Investigations, 1995), pp. 157–166.

24. Palmer, p. 69.

25. Philip Burling, *Crime On Campus: Analyzing and Managing the Increasing Risk of Institutional Liability* (Washington, D.C.: National Association of College and University Attorneys, 1991), pp. 34 and 35.

26. Alan D. MacNutt, "Security/Police Concerns and Needs for Electronic Card Access for Residence Halls", *Campus Law Enforcement Journal,* Vol. 24, No. 6, Nov.Dec., 1994, p. 33.

27. Angie Tipton, "Apartment Inspection Program at the University of Florida," *Campus Law Enforcement Journal,* Vol. 22, No. 6, pp. 32–35.

# Chapter 8

# PHYSICAL/ENVIRONMENTAL SECURITY

## INTRODUCTION

A safe campus environment depends, to some degree on effective physical security measures. The great majority of campuses are not surrounded by fences or walls designed to protect students from the "outside world." Traditionally, many campus facilities have been open around the clock to accommodate special academic needs of students. Many campuses are open to the extent that there is little distinction between campus property and streets and the local neighborhood. Consequently, some colleges and universities wrestle with a wide range of criminal activity committed by intruders from the "outside world." Media accounts of rapes, assaults, burglaries, robberies, theft, and voyeurism perpetrated by nonstudent, outside intruders appear to be increasing. As stated in an earlier discussion, students themselves account for a significant amount of crime on some campuses.

As our nation's crime rate continues to rise, university officials recognize the importance of reducing opportunities for crime on campus and protecting their personnel, equipment, and facilities. Whether the criminals are outside intruders or students, higher education institutions must be reasonably "tamper-proof." It is time that higher education officials take a cue from the modern business and industry world where high tech security and risk management have become necessary priorities. College students deserve to feel safe in their classrooms, residences, and social areas. Campus facilities and equipment should not be easy targets for thieves. As one university public safety administrator states: "Century-old buildings with ivy-covered walls, beautifully grained wooden doors and lush greenery help project a warm and scholarly image for a university, but these qualities do little to provide a safe and secure environment."[1] Creating a truly safe campus will require a definitive philosophy and concomitant policies and programs aimed at reducing the risks to personnel and the physical plant.

124

## Institutional Philosophy and Policies

In general, extensive security barriers which restrict free movement in facilities and around the campus are incompatible with the longstanding beliefs of academic freedom and the educational mission of higher education. Yet, due to the very real threat posed by crime, campus officials must develop a congruent philosophy and reasonable policy that ensures a high level of security while maintaining a relaxed academic and social environment. With careful attention to the primacy of educational values, administrative officials should consider whether it is feasible and advisable to restrict or monitor access of uninvited visitors to their campus. They should take into account how barriers, restrictions, and access control measures will impact the expectations of students as to their freedom and their privileges. There are demonstrable tensions between an ideal academic environment and a completely service campus.[2] Such issues as the degree of security risks posed by visitors, the size and layout of the physical plant, and the extent of risks associated with special events are among those to be considered. A central issue in developing an institutional philosophy is simply whether the campus will be "open" or "closed" to casual visitors. What priority will physical security have in relation to aesthetics, funding, and architectural design?

Policies related to physical and environmental security (includes procedures and guidelines) should be developed with broad participation and dissemination. In keeping with the relatively new community-oriented policing approach, the members of the campus community (students, staff, faculty, and visitors) should be actively involved in policy development and, subsequently, to its implementation. Policies should be written in clear and concise terms. It is recommended that general policies related to the institution's stance on facility security, access control, and the assignment of responsibilities for the various functional categories should be included in an institution-wide policy document which is available to employees. Security policies related to students should be included in a student handbook or other appropriate publication with wide distribution. Policies which pertain to academic building security should be found in appropriate policy documents available to faculty and designated staff. Specific security-related policies for housing facilities should be disseminated to all resident students and housing staff. The campus police/security unit should have a working knowledge of all campus security policies and procedures. While physical security is a shared responsibility across campus, police and security officers are usually first responders and have the charge of implementing many of the policies.

Success in developing an institutional philosophy about security which is compatible with the mission and "spirit" of the institution and its traditions depends on strong leadership at or near the top of the organization. While demands of fiscal accountability, faculty unrest, and enrollment decline are high priorities for college presidents, student safety and liability risks must receive adequate attention and support. College and university presidents should ensure that institutions' philosophies and policies support an equitable balance between an open environment and a protected sanctuary where inquirers can feel secure.

## RISK ASSESSMENT AND PLANNING

Physical/environmental security is often neglected at some colleges and universities. Typically, these institutions provide police/security officers who wander aimlessly about campus, lock buildings, and respond to calls for service. They approach crime prevention in a reactive mode rather than in a proactive one. Physical security should be a priority and may, in fact, be the best deterrent to crime. Security expert Randy Gonzalez, defined physical security as "those efforts which are directed toward the anticipation, recognition, appraisal, and implementation of measures to reduce or eliminate potential crime risks, or breach of security."[3]

Oscar Newman, an urban planner in the early 1970s, developed a theory of defensible space as a response to crime in public housing projects. These principles are applicable to any similar populated environment such as a college campus. Newman's theory involves more than just lights and locks. He believed that physical design can evoke psychological reactions by residents to create a social fabric that defends itself. He also felt that architecture could either encourage or discourage people from taking an active part in their own security. Four major design ingredients are involved in Newman's concept. First, both real and symbolic barriers should be used to subdivide the environment into manageable zones that encourage occupants to assume territorial attitudes. Second, opportunities for surveillance of all areas, by occupants should be maximized. Third, sites should be designed so that occupants are not perceived as vulnerable. Fourth, residential structures should be placed in proximity to safe or nonthreatening areas.[4]

Prior to the development of physical/environmental security programs, campus officials should carefully determine the scope and extent of security problems and needs. A thorough risk or vulnerability assessment process is essential for this. By conducting a comprehensive assessment or audit, officials at all levels will have a clear picture and better understanding of the issues related to security risks.

The assessment should include a review or inspection of the following areas:

A. Landscape
B. Lighting Conditions (Interior & Exterior)
C. Campus Perimeter Access
D. Adjoining Neighborhoods
E. Adjacent/Nearby Environmental Conditions
F. Campus Facilities Security Measures & Access Control
G. Parking Lots and Garages
H. Fences, Walls, and Barriers
I. Existing Security Devices
J. Existing Crime Prevention Measures
K. Existing Policies, Procedures, and Practices
L. Retail Operations On Campus
M. Traffic Access, and Flow
N. Special Needs Operations (Health Care, Computer Center, Research Labs, etc.)

The campus vulnerability audit should be conducted by both professionals and by the users themselves such as staff members, faculty, and students. This process should be directed by a designated official or committee with the authority to accomplish the task. An outside consultant may be used to conduct a needs assessment or to serve as a facilitator for the process. Some institutions conduct risk surveys via a campus environmental and safety committee. It is also recommended that a standard assessment or inspection form be utilized for all offices, buildings, and units on campus with a special addendum for unique categories (i.e., scientific laboratories, health care units, etc.).

When the risk or vulnerability assessment process is completed, the results should be compiled and analyzed for further review. Statistics and conclusions will be helpful in determining trends, special problems, and needs. General recommendations should also accompany the report and should be useful as a starting point for the planning process which should follow. A final report should be disseminated to all participating units and to key institutional officials.

With the completion risk assessment project, immediate steps should be taken to begin a comprehensive planning process to develop ways and means for improving physical/environmental security measures on campus. Key players for this broad-based process should include physical plant/maintenance personnel, police/security officials, risk management staff, faculty representatives, environmental safety officers, campus engineers, housing officials, campus planners, and facilities management staff. Outside expertise may be invited to include local police managers, city management staff, security specialists, and other individuals with special knowledge pertinent to the task of developing an effective physical/environmental security plan. A planning team should be established and charged with developing an effective security plan.

The planning process can begin with the development of goals and objectives. The institutions existing philosophy and policies related to security issues will be helpful in guiding the planning team toward its objectives. The team's next task is to identify and choose acceptable and feasible strategies for achieving each objective. The strategies must be supported with realistic and available resources and time lines. Individual units and officers which may be assigned responsibilities (i.e., public safety, housing, maintenance, etc.) should be directly involving in this process at least in review as it pertains to that unit. Unique questions and issues will likely arise during this process such as: "Is this program or measure cost effective?" or "Is this strategy compatible with the unit's mission and available resources?"

Ultimately the success of a physical/environmental security program will be determined to a large extent by the degree of community participation in the planning process and in the support and involvement in its implementation. Crime prevention planning is an ongoing process which requires the campus community to continually evaluate the effectiveness of programs and modify plans accordingly. Every institution of higher education should designate one office or an official to be responsible for the development of and maintenance of a campus-wide physical/environmental security plan. This plan may also incorporate office safety, emergency response, severe weather, building evaluation, and other related public safety issues.

## STRATEGIES FOR PHYSICAL SECURITY

While this discussion is not intended to be an in-depth treatment of physical security programming, it does offer a compendium of strategies aimed at enhancing campus safety and security. College and university officials should recognize the importance of addressing these issues on the front end and instead of discovering the outcomes on the back end. Campus physical security is and has been recognized as an item on the national higher-education agenda. In October, 1985, the American Council on Education endorsed a set of campus security-related initiatives developed by its Advisory Committee for Self-Regulation Initiatives. The executive Committee of the American College Personnel Association also endorsed the document in July, 1985. These initiatives include recommendations for enhancing campus physical and environmental security. In part, these recommendations include:

1. Restrict and monitor access to campus grounds
2. Periodically examine grounds-keeping standards from a security point of view to include building entrances, parking areas, outdoor communications facilities, and major pathways with respect to landscaping which may detract from security.
3. Periodically review the adequacy of outdoor campus lighting.
4. Maintain and document adequate procedures for key control.[5]

The following sections address specific areas and issues which are considered essential components of an effective physical/environmental security program. Sound practices and strategies are offered to assist higher education officials in creating a safe campus.

### Perimeter Security and Access Control

College campuses come in many varieties and geographic configurations. Some campuses have easily defined boundaries while others may be undistinguishable from the city streets and buildings which surround them. However, most universities have some kind of property lines and boundaries which can be recognized as campus-owned property. This distinction in campus property becomes particularly important when legal issues are raised such as duty of care, liability, and foreseeability. Consequently, it is important that university officials become especially concerned about campus perimeter security and the level of access control which the institution exercises.

While campus rules and regulations which apply to students and employees of the institution may have some deterrent effect, they are much less persuasive in deterring criminal behavior by outsiders. Whether these outsiders be legitimate visitors or intruders, they may be ignorant of and/or have little regard for campus rules. In fact, some public safety directors report that outsiders consider students and campus property as "easy prey." There are many media accounts of college students being murdered, raped, robbed, and assaulted on campus by nonstudent outsiders. For example, in 1986, a star football player at Florida State University was shot and killed on campus by a nonstudent. The FSU student, six-foot-five Pablo Lopez died of a shotgun blast to the abdomen during a fight with a nonstudent.

Can institutions construct barriers around the campus sufficient to keep out intruders? Realistically, most cannot. However, awareness of the potential threats created by unrestricted access should be the catalyst for developing strategies which will result in improved monitoring and access control.

The ultimate access control strategy would be a high perimeter away around the entire campus with restricted and controlled entrance gates. This is exactly the level of perimeter security employed at Birmingham-Southern College in Birmingham, Alabama. Because of several intrusion incidents and serious crimes near the campus, officials there erected a ten-foot iron and brick fence around the campus. Access to campus is restricted, with special exceptions, to one main gate. This gate is manned on a 24-hour basis by armed, uniformed security officers. It has proven successful not only in reducing outside intrusion but creates a sense of security among students.

There are less restrictive, yet, effective access control measures which are common to many institutions. Limiting vehicular access to one or two entrances will offer a degree of control. It affords police/security officers the opportunity to monitor all vehicles as they enter and leave the campus. An option to this strategy is to have officers check the identification of all drivers and passengers. While students may simply verify their status either by picture identification or automobile registration, nonstudents may be required to provide more information or even to sign in and out.

In lieu of stopping vehicles at gates, surveillance cameras may be utilized. These cameras can monitor designated campus entrances for vehicles as well as pedestrians. A central monitoring station will permit security personnel to monitor these locations and dispatch officers when suspicion warrants it. The very presence of surveillance cameras can have a deterrent effect on some would-be intruders. Most criminals are less likely to perpetrate crime if they know they are recognized and can be identified.

### Adjoining Neighborhoods and Nearby Environmental Factors

Crime, intrusion, traffic, and noise are just a few of the threats to a safe campus created by adjoining neighborhoods and other nearby environmental factors. In fact, some of these factors may be perpetrated by students living off campus in adjoining neighborhoods. There are some basic assumptions about the social-environmental aspect of the university-community relationship which should be considered. They include:

1. There is a striking difference in nearby neighborhoods, when the university is in session and when students are home for the holidays or summer vacation.
2. At most universities, some students will dwell in off-campus housing.
3. Students' behavior and values will likely be different from that of the local community members.
4. Students' social activities will frequently result in loud music, misconduct, and alcohol-related behavior.
5. In some instances, off-campus rental dwellings in nearby neighborhoods are allowed to deteriorate.
6. The university campus can be detrimentally affected by criminal activity perpetrated by local residents.
7. High-volume traffic routes, large industrial complexes, and urban encroachment are factors which can negatively impact the campus environment.

As discussed in the preceding section, perimeter security and enhanced access control measures may reduce the risks and impacts associated with these environmental conditions. However, in some cases perimeter security may either not be possible or it may not be the appropriate solution. Enhancing physical/environmental security for the campus may require more innovative programming than simply physical security measures.

During the 1970s, Vanderbilt University in Nashville, Tennessee experienced problems with an adjacent community. High crime, low income, and other problems plagued not only the neighborhood but often impacted Vandy students. In cooperation with local city officials, Vanderbilt developed an urban renewal program and was able through eminent domain procedures to seize some local deteriorating property. This area was subsequently transformed into more value property. Ultimately, the negative impact and threat created on the campus was diminished.[6]

Another model strategy can be found at the University of Notre Dame. Officials there have demonstrated their commitment to reducing the risks of criminal activity for students on and near the main campus. The Northeast Neighborhood Project provides for the revitalization of a crime-ravaged neighborhood that formerly housed many off-campus students. The University of Notre Dame worked in a community partnership with South Bend officials to weed out drug dealers and rehabilitate or tear down old apartment buildings. Students moved back into the neighborhood and the University provided some extended police patrols in the area to assist city police.[7]

Threats from adjoining neighborhoods and other nearby impacts should be addressed in conjunction with local government leaders, local residents, and neighborhood associations. All illustrated above, some institutions have even taken proactive steps in dealing with crime in nearby neighborhoods where students live.

**Facility Access Control**

Access control is a basic component of an effective security program. Protection of property and people requires some degree of access control for facilities. Campus crime statistics nationwide reveal that property crime is the most frequently reported type of crime. Some individual universities report more than a thousand burglaries and thefts annually.[8] Crimes against persons where building security is shown to be inadequate are also frequently reported by campus police agencies. University officials are, in fact, becoming increasingly aware of the importance of facility access control.

While the assessment process and initial security planning normally involves existing facilities, many new facilities may not be adequately designed to address security. It is, therefore, wise to avoid facility security problems by having input in the pre-construction, architectural designing phase. Building specifications such as lighting, access, electric wiring, and other aspects should be planned with crime prevention in mind. Security should be an integral part of construction.

Facility access control in nonresidential buildings has become necessary due to significant financial losses due to theft and vandalism. Prior to installing an electronic security system, University of Minnesota (UM) officials reported losing $200,000 a year in computer theft alone. Other targets at UM included microscopes, galleries, vending machines, game rooms, theaters, and video arcades. The University regularly lost thousands of dollars worth of electronic equipment, video cameras, VCR's, CD players, and TV gear. Officials at UM installed a cost-effective wireless detection system in these critical areas and cut their losses to nearly zero.[9]

Whether wireless remote or sophisticated fiberoptic cable systems are used, university officials should protect campus buildings and property with the appropriate security technology. Special nonresidential areas commonly vulnerable to intrusion and theft include ATM's (anytime teller machines), computer labs, libraries, retail operations, and electronic equipment storage areas. Controlling access and monitoring facility use has proven to be a deterrent to unauthorized entry and criminal behavior. Nonresidential facilities are also vulnerable to crimes against persons and should be adequately monitored and controlled. Libraries, classroom buildings (especially night classes), elevators, snackbars, bookstores, and parking garages are areas which should receive special attention by public safety officials. Wireless remote detectors, surveillance cameras, infrared motion detectors, sound sensors, enunciators, photoelectric magnetic switches, microwave, proximity devices, window alarms, audio alarms, and other types of electronic security equipment are all available for appropriate application. It is important that access control devices be properly monitored. It is recommended that the campus police/security operation maintain a 24-hour central monitoring service with police response capability.

In addition to electronic physical security measures, there are other facility construction and design issues which can be addressed even in older, existing buildings. Locking devices, number of access door, roof access, ventilation shafts, wall construction, window construction, and landscaping are some basic areas for concern. Sophisticated security alarms and even security personnel will enhance these basic aspects for facility security.

Residential facility access control is of special significance to those concerned about creating a safe campus since the topic received considerable treatment in a previous chapter, it is sufficient here to reiterate the importance of adequate support to residential security access control. While the level and type of monitoring/control systems should be determined by each institution, effective access control for student housing facilities is no longer optional if officials are genuinely concerned about students' safety and institutional liability.

## Campus Lighting Conditions

Adequate lighting outdoors and in facilities is another critical element in an effective physical/environmental security program. Adequate lighting received special emphasis in the American Council on Education's *Self-Regulation Initiatives* report as follows:

### Adequacy of Outdoor Lighting

A. Each institution should periodically review the adequacy of its outdoor campus lighting from a security point of view.
B. All authorized entrances to student housing buildings should be sufficiently illuminated after dusk to permit observation of persons loitering in the vicinity. Lighting should be distributed about the rest of the campus to cover building entrances, pathways, parking facilities, and other open areas where students must travel after dusk.
C. Each institution should systematically monitor the operation of outdoor lighting. The light-monitoring system should include a program to replace defective or burnt-out lights as soon as practical after being reported.[10]

The first step in determining campus lighting needs is to conduct a lighting survey. This may be done with the assistance of an outside security consultant or campus officials may conduct a comprehensive assessment using some expert knowledge base. Campus engineers, security specialists, and electrical utility technicians are among those who may already be available on campus. Based on the results of the survey, a campus lighting plan should be developed and implemented in a timely manner.

As outlined in the ACE report, the amount of illumination should be sufficient in all areas where students, visitors, and employees are likely to walk or drive. These include parking areas, walkways, classrooms, common areas of buildings, around buildings, in and around athletic facilities, recreation areas, and around facility entrances and exits. Amble lighting should also be placed near the perimeter of the campus. The appropriate amount of illumination (measured in candle power) should be installed—especially in high-risk areas such as parks, jogging tracks, and adjacent to off-campus problem areas.

A well-lighted campus will create a sense of safety among students and likely serve as a deterrent to intruders. Campus police, maintenance personnel, housing officials, and other campus officials should develop and sustain a reporting procedure for inoperative lighting devices as well as perceived areas of need for lighting.

## Grounds and Landscaping

Exterior campus areas should receive special attention from public safety and physical plant officials. While most institutions of higher education commit extensive funds and efforts to beautify their landscapes and physical plant, care should be taken not to create security hazards. Physical/environmental security issues particularly relate to groundskeeping practices, landscaping, and visibility. These areas should be evaluated and approached with a safety and security perspective. New building construction and landscape modification should always involve security inspection early in the process. Existing building modifications, parking lot changes, street construction, and other changes in the physical plant should require a close examination of their impact on security.

Foliage such as shrubs should be kept trimmed so that they do not provide cover for prowling, voyeurism, and attacks. The height of shrubs should be kept relatively low to negate opportunities for concealment. Trees should also be kept trimmed from the bottom up so that limbs and leaves do not create blind areas conducive to hiding.

Fences, walls, and other man-made barriers should be evaluated for their security factors, whether positive or negative. Ideally, this should always be a consideration prior to construction of the barriers.

The general landscape and terrain should be viewed from a security point of view. Ditches, mounds, and piles of leaves, snow, and other debris should be considered as potential security hazards. Any such area which diminishes good visibility and negates the effects of proper illumination should be modified if possible.

Shrubs, trees, and terrain factors should especially be modified or even removed where their presence may create concealment near walkways, roadways, residence halls, and other campus buildings. As discussed in a previous section, proper illumination on these areas will offer additional safety and security enhancement.

A good ongoing security inspection should include assessment of grounds and landscaping. Inspection reports should be directed at those responsible for taking corrective action in a timely manner. Prior to new construction projects, expansions, and modifications to facilities or grounds, a safety/security impact study should be conducted.

An additional security approach related to outdoor areas on campus is that of security or emergency call boxes. These may utilize regular line-operated telephones with a single push-button feature or more recently the use of cellular call devices is found at several institutions. These emergency call devices should be located throughout the campus grounds and be monitored by police/security personnel.

**Parking Areas**

Perhaps the area considered the most vulnerable for such incidents as assaults, robberies, and automobile burglaries is parking lots and garages. These areas often provide opportunities for crime because of their characteristics. Large numbers of automobiles parked close together offer excellent concealment for perpetrators. Parking lots are often located in remote areas or a significant distance from buildings. Parking garages and multistory parking decks worsen the situation since building support pillars and other barriers offer cover for intruders. Automobiles also provide the opportunity for attackers to control victims inside the vehicles. The contents often left visible in automobiles create prime targets for perpetrators to burglarize and steal. Nighttime hours is a particularly vulnerable time for students and employees to enter and exit their vehicles in parking areas.

On November 4, 1990, a Duke University female employee was attacked and shot five times in a University parking garage. Despite on-duty security personnel, the employee's estranged husband was successful in entering her car and critically wounding her before fatally shooting himself.

On December 14, 1994, two Jacksonville State University students were carjacked and one of them shot in the buttocks as they loaded their car to go home for the Christmas Holidays. Two suspects, believed to be nonstudents, fled in the victims' car.

These are examples of hundreds of crimes which occur each year in campus parking areas. While most institutions have increased security, lighting, and developed elaborate crime prevention programs, parking lot security remains an area which cries for more efforts.

Parking areas should be very well lighted. High-mast, clustered, reflector-style lighting has proven to be effective. Some parking areas can be well illuminated by 1,000-watt mercury or metal-halide reflectorized lamps mounted on a single multiheaded mast 100 feet high. Such lighting is estimated to illuminate an area as large as four football fields. This type of lighting cuts down on the need for a large number of poles or masts. They are also high enough to be relatively safe from vandals.[11] Sodium vapor lights were installed in parking areas at Bates College in Maine. They increased illumination by 30 percent and at a lower cost than the previous lighting system.[12]

As part of a $7.5 million multilevel parking project, the University of Minnesota, Minneapolis, incorporated audio and visual surveillance, card access, motion detection, and emergency call buttons into its parking security program—a system which serves 40,000 students, 40 percent of whom commute to campus everyday. A fixed-camera CCTV system monitors the new garage's four-stair towers, elevator lobbies, elevator cabs, and all ingress and egress points. Color cameras were installed at exit and access points for improved clarity in case an incident calls for an enhanced photo for motorist or vehicle identification. The cameras also either include motion, detection, audio, or threshold alarms. Call buttons were also installed at each stair landing and in each elevator cab in order to provide immediate communication with parking officials. A central control center allows security personnel to monitor all security alarms and devices.[13]

Call boxes or push-button emergency devices as mentioned in the previous section on grounds, should be considered for use in all parking areas—especially those which are in remote locations. These emergency call buttons or telephones should be well identified, easy to locate, and easy to operate. They should be monitored by security personnel and receive a priority status for police response. The types of these devices vary. However, there is a variety of types and prices which have broad application not only for parking areas but also for interior areas, elevators, walking areas, and remote areas of the campus.

## SUMMARY

Physical/environmental security is becoming a more important concern for campus officials. Due to increased incidents of crime and violence on campuses across the nation, it is foreseeable that intrusion and crime will occur. College and university presidents should reexamine their existing physical plant security conditions. Comprehensive assessments and planning should result in upgrading security procedures and physical measures throughout the campus.

In this age of advanced technology there is an ample supply of innovative programs and sophisticated devices with direct application for campus physical security. Additional, there are many less expensive, practical modifications which are available to campus officials. Grounds, landscaping, parking areas, lighting, and perimeter access are factors which must be examined for possible enhancements.

Students expect and deserve to feel safe on their campuses. Environmental security measures serve as the frontline defense for protected campus residents. In survey after survey an unacceptable percentage of students respond that they do not feel safe on campus. Every feasible approach should be used to reduce the risks and deter criminal behavior. Students will recognize and appreciate legitimate efforts to create a safe campus environment.

## ENDNOTES

1. John R. Haelig, "Ensuring security through construction and design." *Campus Law Enforcement Journal*, Vol. 19, No. 6, November/December 1988, p. 38.

2. American Council on Education, *Self-Regulation Initiatives: Resource Documents for Colleges and Universities* (Washington D.C.: American Council on Education: 1985).

3. Randy Gonzalez, *Developing Crime Prevention and Physical Security Planning For the College and University Environment*, (Holmes Beach, Florida: Crime Prevention and Physical Security Planning Publications, 1986), p. 3.

4. Michael Clay Smith and Richard Fossey, *Crime on Campus: Legal Issues and Campus Administration*, (Phoenix, Arizona: American Council On Education Oryx Press, 1995), pp. 68 & 69.

5. American Council on Education, *Initiatives*.

6. David Nichols, *University-Community Relations: Living Together Effectively*, (Springfield, Illinois: Charles C Thomas Publisher, 1990), p. 97.

7. *Campus Crime*, (Business Publishers, Inc., Silver Springs, Maryland, 1994) Vol. 4, No. 7, p. 67.

8. Uniform Crime Reports for 1994, U.S. Department of Justice (U.S. Government Printing Office, Washington, D.C., 1994), pp. 157–166.

9. Jim Gregory, "Wireless Electronic Security at the University of Minnesota," *Campus Law Enforcement Journal*, Vol. 24, No. 6, November/December 1994, pp. 30–32.

10. American Council On Education, *Initiatives*.

11. John W. Powell, Michael S. Ponder, and Robert C. Nielsen, *Campus Security and Law Enforcement*, (Boston, Massachusetts: Butterworth-Heinemann, 1994), p. 157.

12. Connie J. Kirkland and Dorothy S. Siegel, *Campus Security: A First Look at Promising Practices,* (Washington, D.C.: Office of Educational Research and Improvement, U.S. Department of Education, 1994), p. 22.

13. *Campus Security Report,* (Port Washington, New York: Rusting Publications, 1995) Vol. 7, Number 7, July 1995, p. 13.

# Chapter 9

# RECORDS, REPORTING, AND DISCLOSURE

## INTRODUCTION

American higher education has historically been characterized by a unique degree of privacy and protection from the outside world. As discussed earlier in this book, colleges and universities were once considered sanctuaries apart from the real world. Part of this notion included a "nobody's business" philosophy to handling institution affairs, especially those which might bring reproach on the good name and image of the school. These "dirty laundry" issues such as student misconduct, acts of miscreant employees, and criminal incidents were, by and large, considered private matters to be dealt with through internal measures. Crime on America's college and university campuses, particularly violent crime, has been described as one of the best kept secrets of modern times.[1] This seemed to be acceptable until the late 1970s and early 1980s when an increase in campus crime, alcohol abuse, illegal drugs, accidents, and other threats to safe campuses became widely known. Public awareness, litigation, and fears of students and parents caught the attention of lawmakers and the media. News reports of serious crimes such as murder, rape, and robbery on one campus after another created a furor which has forced college and university officials to change the way they handle many serious criminal incidents and the way they protect their students.

Today, exemplary campus safety-related programs can be found at many colleges and universities of all categories. These programs are aimed at informing students of potential risks and available measures for their assistance. Particularly important are recent federally mandated requirements which direct institutions of higher education to maintain reporting systems for the campus community and to disclose specified information to students and the public. Most recently, some "sacred cows" such as student disciplinary records have come under scrutiny in terms of their protection from disclosure.

Despite the arguments against revealing student-perpetrated acts of

140

violence and other misconduct and despite the reluctance of administrators of some schools to release potentially negative information, progress toward creating safer campuses is evident. Through a series of laws and regulations at both the federal and state level, better informed students and parents can choose institutions which demonstrate a commitment to safety and security issues.

## PROGRAM MANDATES AND REPORTING OBLIGATIONS

There are a number of states which have passed meaningful legislation aimed at enhancing safety and security on college campuses. These laws relate to such issues as crime statistics reporting, illegal drugs, alcohol violations, and firearms. Administrators should be familiar with campus security-related laws in their individual states. However, this discussion will focus on two major federally mandated laws which pertain to campus safety and security: (1) The Drug-Free Schools and Communities Act Amendments of 1989 and (2) The Crime Awareness and Campus Security Act of 1990.

## DRUG–FREE SCHOOLS AND CAMPUSES

President George Bush's National Drug Control Strategy issued in September, 1989, proposed that the Congress pass legislation to require schools, colleges, and universities to implement and enforce firm drug prevention programs and policies as a condition of eligibility to receive Federal financial assistance. On December 12, 1989, President Bush signed the Drug-Free Schools and Communities Act Amendments of 1989, (Public Law 101-226.)[2]

The problems associated with alcohol and other drugs have become excessive and unacceptable. The Commission on Substance Abuse at Colleges and Universities, established by the Center on Addiction and Substance Abuse (CASA) at Columbia University, found evidence that excessive drinking puts students at high-risk for AIDS, rape, violence, and unplanned pregnancies. One in three college students—most of them underage—now drink primarily to get drunk. According to the Commission, colleges and universities pay the price for the widespread alcohol abuse on their campuses:[3]

1. Ninety-five percent of violent crimes and 53 percent of all injuries on campus are alcohol-related.
2. Alcohol is implicated in some 41 percent of all academic problems.
3. Each year, students spend over $5.5 billion on alcoholic beverages; more than they spend on all other drinks and books combined.
4. Ninety percent of all campus rapes occur when alcohol is being used either by the assailant, the victim, or both.

Many college officials once hesitated to articulate clear alcohol and other drug policies on the assumption that these policies, because they could not be perfectly enforced, would contribute to the institution's liability in a court of law. As a result, policies at these schools, if they existed at all, were limited to recitations of relevant state and local laws.

School officials can no longer justify this stance. First, the Drug-Free Schools and Communities Act Amendments of 1989 now require schools to develop, announce, and enforce an unequivocal set of policies for preventing the misuse of alcohol and other drugs on campus. Second, a number of court rulings have made clear that, while schools cannot be expected to control student conduct, they must ensure that their activities and programs meet reasonable standards of care, and they must take steps to deal with potentially and foreseeable dangerous situations on campus. Meeting these requirements means having clear rules and a standard of firm and consistent enforcement. One area which creates substantial risk and requires special programming is that of alcohol and drug abuse on campus.

While college administrators have for some time become concerned about student alcohol and other drug use, the driving force behind recent preventive activity has been the passage of the Drug-Free Schools and Communities Act Amendments of 1989, coupled with the availability of prevention grant monies through the Fund for Improvement of Postsecondary Education (FIPSE) administered by the U.S. Department of Education. The 1989 Amendments require that every institution of higher education, as a condition of receiving any Federal financial assistance, must communicate the following information to each student and employee:

(1) "Standards of conduct that clearly prohibit the unlawful possession, use, or distribution of illicit drugs and alcohol by students and employees on its property or as part of its activities."
(2) "A clear statement that the institution will impose sanctions on students and employees (consistent with local, State, and Federal law), and a description of

those sanctions, up to and including expulsion or termination of employment and referred for prosecution, for violations of the standards of conduct."

In addition, schools are required to review their prevention program every two years to assess effectiveness and ensure that disciplinary sanctions are being enforced consistently. Any school that fails to take reasonable steps to enforce these required policies places itself at risk of losing federal funds.

The 1989 Amendments establish a minimum set of requirements for college substance use policies. Some college administrators mistakenly believe that this Federal statute is the only basis for their legal responsibilities in this regard. It does so, in part. Another catalyst for improved alcohol and drug policies is recent court rulings in negligence suits against colleges and universities. The courts have become increasingly sympathetic to plaintiffs who have sued third parties for damage caused by someone who has been drinking. Most legal analysts agree that colleges and universities are increasingly in danger of being sued for property damage or injuries that result from student drinking.

Colleges and universities should develop effective alcohol/drug prevention and assistance programs. These should be available to both students and employees. Student health services, counseling centers, crisis intervention offices, and others should provide services for the campus community. Further campus law enforcement and judicial officials should ensure consistent enforcement of written sanctions.

## Campus Security Act of 1990

On November 8, 1990, President George Bush signed into law the Student Right-to-Know and Campus Security Act (Public Law 101-542). On April 29, 1994, the U.S. Department of Education issued the final regulations pertaining to the Campus Security Act. Largely through the efforts of Howard and Constance Cleary, whose daughter was brutally raped and murdered in her Lehigh University dormitory room in 1986, the issue of campus crime has been brought to the attention of the national media, several state legislatures, and the U.S. Congress. Their efforts were bolstered by support from leading campus law enforcement officials. The impacts of the Act are far-reaching, affecting every post-secondary institution in the nation which receives Federal Title IV funds (student financial aid). Its findings include: (1) Violent crime on campus has steadily increased in recent years; (2) 95 percent of violent crime on campus are alcohol or drug related; (3) 80 percent of campus crimes are committed by students on other students: and (4) There is a clear need for institutions to develop security policies and procedures and to report them.

Through the Campus Security Act, Congress expressed a new policy objective. This objective essentially states that the public has the right to obtain information about campus crime, including crimes that involve students. In passing this Act, Congress imposed sweeping obligations on higher education institutions to gather information about crimes that occur on their campuses and to make this information available to students, employees, and the public.[4] Further, there are mandated policy, program, and procedure requirements related to campus crime and security measures.

Institutions receiving Title IV student aid assistance are required to provide two types of reporting requirements. First, according to the statute and regulations, colleges and universities are required to prepare and distribute by September 1 of each year an annual campus security report which sets forth its policies and gives statistics on a number of specified crimes—murder, forcible or nonforcible sex offenses (including rape), robbery, aggravated assault, burglary, and motor vehicle theft. Also, statistics for specified arrests are required to include liquor law violations, drug abuse violations, and weapons possessions. This report must be distributed to all current students and employees, and upon request, to applicants for enrollment or employment. Also, when requested, must submit a copy of this annual report to the U.S. Secretary of Education.

Second, the regulations require colleges and universities to provide *timely warnings* to the campus community of the six specified crimes that are reported to campus security authorities or local law enforcement and which may be considered a threat to other students and/or employees. In determining how to inform students and employees about threats and dangerous incidents, campus officials should review and determine effective approaches. These might include press releases, special notices in residence facilities, fliers, posters, telephone calls, and/or mailings.

The regulations define a campus as "(i) any building or property owned or controlled by the institution of higher education within the same reasonably contiguous geographic area and used by the institution in direct support of, or in a manner related to, the institution's educational purposes; (ii) any building or property owned or controlled by a student organization recognized by the institution; or (iii) any building or property controlled by the institution, but owned by a third party." Branch campuses, schools, or divisions that are not within a reasonably contiguous geographic area are considered separate campuses for reporting purposes.

In most cases, fraternity, sorority, and other organizational housing units will be considered part of the campus regardless of location and ownership. Other areas that may be included as part of the campus are recreation/camp sites, research facilities, and teaching hospitals.[5]

Under the Act's general reporting requirements that apply to campus crime, colleges and universities must include in their annual security reports the following policy information:

> Current campus policies regarding procedures and facilities for students and others to report criminal actions and other emergencies occurring on campus, policies concerning the institution's response to the reports, and a list of the titles of each person or organization to whom students and employees should report the criminal offenses.

> Examples might include the availability of campus security, the existence of a network of emergency telephones, publication and promotion of emergency phone numbers, and orientation programs.

> Current policies concerning security of and access to campus facilities, including residences, and security considerations related to maintenance programs.

> Examples might include policies governing access to academic buildings, residence halls, fraternities and sororities, and other facilities; and the procedure for inspecting campus lighting and shrubbery.

> Current policies concerning campus law enforcement, including the enforcement authority of institutional security personnel, their relationship with state and local police agencies, law enforcement (arrest) authority of campus security personnel, and policies that encourage prompt reporting of all campus crime to the campus police and local police.

> Examples might include: Does campus security have law enforcement authority? What is the nature of the working relationship between campus security and local law enforcement agencies?

> A description of the type and frequency of programs designed to (1) inform students and employees about campus security procedures, (2) inform students and employees about the prevention of crimes, and (3) encourage students and employees to be responsible for their own security and the security of others. The description of the program should include reference to the manner in which the campus will provide a "timely warning notice" of violent crimes reported to campus or local police that are considered to be a threat to students and employees. Institutions are encouraged to specify that such action will depend on the particular circumstances of the crime.

Examples of types of programs colleges and universities could offer to students and employees might include orientation programs, residence hall education programs, campus safety awareness programs, and employee training and handbooks.

Policy concerning the monitoring and recording by local police agencies of students' criminal activity at student organizations' off-campus locations, including off-campus housing facilities.

Policy regarding the possession, use, or sale of alcoholic beverages and illegal drugs, as well as any drug and alcohol abuse education programs required by the Drug-Free and Communities Amendments of 1989 (Public Law 101-226).

This section will require the institution to summarize or reference the information already required by the Drug-Free Schools and Communities Act.

The regulations also mandate the adoption of certain institutional policies specific to sex offenses. Analogous to the general security—related policy statements above, the sex-related policies promote the importance of encouraging sex crime victims to report offenses and mandate campus procedures to facilitate such reporting. The institution's statement of policy must include the following information:[6]

Education programs designed to promote awareness of rape, acquaintance rape, and other forcible or nonforcible sex offenses.

Procedures students should follow if a sex offense occurs, including who should be contacted, the importance of preserving evidence as it may be necessary for the proof of a criminal sexual offense, and to whom the alleged offense should be reported.

We urge institutions to consult with their campus security officials, local law enforcement officials, and the local prosecutor's office when addressing what constitutes the preservation of evidence.

The student's option to notify proper law enforcement authorities, including on-campus and local police, and the option to be assisted by campus authorities in notifying these authorities if the student chooses to do so.

Existing on-and-off-campus counseling, mental health, or other student services for victims of sexual offenses.

Notification to students that the institution will change a victim's academic and living situations after an alleged sex offense and of the options for those changes, if requested by the victim and if the changes are reasonably available.

Institutions are not required to make a change of accommodations if the request by a victim is unreasonable. For example, an institution could allow a victim out of a housing contract with the institution so that the student may pursue off-campus housing, but it would not be reasonable to expect the institution to pay for the rental of a private apartment for the student.

Procedures for on-campus disciplinary actions in cases of alleged sexual offense that shall include a clear statement that: (i) the accuser and the accused are entitled to the same opportunities to have others present during a campus disciplinary proceeding; and (ii) both the accuser and the accused shall be informed of the outcome of any campus disciplinary proceedings brought alleging a sex offense.

Sanctions the institution may impose for rape, acquaintance rape, or other sex offenses (forcible or nonforcible) following an on-campus disciplinary procedure.

## RECORDS AND DISCLOSURE

Colleges and universities create and maintain a wide variety of records pertaining to students. These may include academic records, health records, financial records, admission records, disciplinary records, and criminal incident-related records. The last two of these—disciplinary records and criminal incident-related records—relate to student conduct and present complex issues for higher education officials. These issues are somewhat complicated further due to several factors. As discussed earlier in this chapter, institutions were once unencumbered with any formal record-keeping and reporting obligation outside the institution. Another factor is that institutions generally handled most all student misconduct within the private campus judicial process even though some acts of misconduct constituted serious criminal behavior. Also, until recent history, few colleges or universities had any resemblance of bonified police officers on campus and, consequently, had no police records with which to maintain. And finally, recent federal legislation now calls for the disclosure of specified information and, thus, create the need for new policies, procedures, and approaches.

Student disciplinary records and student crime records have become the focus of much debate. Proponents of strict privacy to these records argue that they should be protected as educational records and not punitive or criminal in nature. Open records advocates view this as an effort to cover up serious crime and inculcate the institution from the truth about campus crime. The competing natures of public records and student privacy rights may clash when it comes to campus crime. Most public records and other official activities are open to public scrutiny under so-called sunshine laws and federal and state freedom of information statues. The citizenry's "right to know" is zealously asserted by the news media. At the same time, some state education laws protect student privacy, all those concerned with educational administration are aware of the pervasive presence of the Family Rights and Privacy Act (FERPA), often referred to as the Buckley Amendment.[7]

## FERPA'S Impact

In essence, the Buckley Amendment prevents educational institutions from releasing personally identifiable information in what it calls, "educational records" about a student to most third parties without the student's permission. Recent changes to federal campus crime laws (Campus Security Act) have broadened the circumstances in which disclosure is permissible. Effective February 25, 1993, FERPA was amended to "allow institutions of postsecondary education to disclose the results of a disciplinary proceeding conducted by the institution against an alleged perpetrator of a crime of violence to the alleged victim of that crime without the prior written consent of the alleged perpetrator."

In addition, the Buckley Amendment does not extend to "records maintained by a law enforcement unit of the educational agency or institution that were created by that law enforcement unit for the purpose of law enforcement." The exception for law enforcement records "neither requires nor prohibits the release of such records, but allows institutions to make choices in light of state laws." As a result, the identity of the accuser and the accused may be vulnerable to disclosure if public access is sought from campus police records under state freedom of information or other state laws. Legal counsel should be consulted regarding the application of other state laws that affect victims' and arrested persons' rights, including state statutes specifically pertaining to rights of persons involved in sex crimes.[8]

## Challenges To Open Records

There have been several attempts to gain access to student disciplinary records. During the early 1990s, some student newspapers pressed for access to student disciplinary hearings and records. The Student Press Law Center, an advocacy group in Washington, D.C., and organizations of professional journalists promote greater access to student disciplinary records. Two lawsuits, against the University of Georgia and Louisiana State University in Shreveport, were decided with different outcomes.

At Georgia, *The Red and Black*, a privately supported student paper, sued the University to gain access to the records of two cases against fraternities involving allegations of hazing. At Louisiana State at Shreveport, a reporter on the student newspaper and a representative of the Society of Professional Journalists sued the University seeking access to records involving allegations of financial misconduct by student government officers.

In a narrowly focused ruling, the Georgia Supreme Court held that the records of the two hearings on hazing should be made available to the public, under state statutes governing open meetings and open records. In Red and Black Publishing Company v. Board of Regents (427 S.E. 2d 257 GA. 1993), the court ruled that the records were not "educational records" but more akin to records kept for law enforcement purposes. The decision implied that the Buckley Amendment does not protect students' disciplinary records from release. Following the decision, the Attorney General of Georgia ordered state colleges and universities to open all disciplinary hearings and records.

In the Louisiana case, a state court ruled in favor of the university's attempts to keep disciplinary records confidential. The court ruled that although the hearings and records sought were covered by the public records laws, they were protected from release under the right to privacy guaranteed by the Louisiana Constitution.[9]

The debate as to whether campus judicial proceedings should be open records and not covered under "education records" will likely end up in Congress. In January 1995, the Department of Education issued a statement which said Congress should decide because the implications of the federally-mandated FERPA legislation was created by Congress.[10] At present, the Department of Education's position is that student disciplinary records and hearings fall under "educational records" and not "law enforcement records." In its final rules, the Education Department amended FERPA regulations to include "disciplinary actions or proceedings" as "educational records" (FERPA, 60 Fed. Reg. 3464), thereby preventing the disclosure of disciplinary proceedings or actions.[11]

In a similar challenge to campus crime records, FERPA was explicitly raised as a defense by school officials. In Baurer v. Kincaid, 759 F. Supp. 575 (W.D. Mo. 1991) student newspaper editor Tracy Baker sued Southwest Missouri State University after it refused to give her access to a campus security department incident report involving an accusation of sexual assault against a student athlete. The school relied on FERPA for denying access. The court ruled that FERPA's definition of "educational records" was not intended to include crime reports, but if it had been the intent of Congress, the law would be unconstitutional as a violation of the First and Fifth Amendments.

## A MODEL REPORTING PROGRAM

In 1993, Syracuse University implemented an enhanced disclosure and reporting program for crime-related incidents. In response to student complaints and accusations related to underreporting and mishandling cases of rape and assault on campus, the chancellor appointed a 15-member Task Force On Student Rights and Responsibilities. The Task Force was comprised of students, faculty members, and administrators and they were charged with developing recommendations in three areas—confidentiality of student records, university judicial proceedings, and reporting of rape and sexual assault statistics. Upon completion of a thorough study and analysis of finding, the Task Force submitted its recommendations to the chancellor. The approved recommendations are as follows:

1. *Publish monthly statistics and dispositions of rape and sexual assault cases.* All sex offense cases reported to campus police, local police, and the R.A.P.E. Center are published along with the disposition of related campus judicial proceedings.
2. *Immediate Notice.* In the case of an incident of one or more offenses which poses a threat to the campus community, immediate release of information by campus security seems essential and is required by Federal Law. These potential threats should be placed in campus newspapers, in fliers around campus, and electronic mail.
3. *Expanded Annual Reports.* In addition to covering university-owned property in federally-mandated crime statistics reports, the Task Force encouraged the University to cover off-campus areas commonly perceived as part of the campus.
4. *Improve Educational Initiatives.* More coordination, program expansion, and extended coverage of related issues such as alcohol's role in nonconsensual sexual activity. Make efforts to increase participation in a university-wide crime prevention effort.
5. *Improve the Reporting Procedures for Victims.* Enhance the relationship and reporting between the R.A.P.E. Center and campus security as well as continue to establish strong linkages with local police which serve student crime victims at off-campus locations.
6. *Additional Recommendations:* (1) train judicial board members about sexual assault; (2) retain existing policies which provide confidentiality for university judicial system proceedings; and (3) offer more education about the role of drug and alcohol consumption in relation to rape and sexual assault.

Of particular significance about this process is the degree of support from the chancellor and from many other officials within the campus community. Student participation and representation is an essential component for this effort to be successful. And finally, in addition to the time and efforts of all involved, there is additional funding to support these recommendations.[12]

## SUMMARY

In today's litigious climate, higher education officials must sometimes walk a tightrope when balancing the rights and privacy of students with the long-held freedom of information rights. Care should be exercised when handling students disciplinary matters. Campus public safety officials should understand their legal obligations as well as restrictions on releasing crime-related information. Institutions which have their own campus police and security units should have those records maintained separately from other "education records" to include student disciplinary processes and records. Campus judicial officials should ensure strict confidentiality of all proceedings and records. When in doubt, legal consultation should be sought.

Campus crime reporting is important in creating a safe campus. Students and employees should be aware of foreseeable threats and have a clear understanding of policies, procedures, and measures available to them. The Right to Know and Campus Security Act has already had an impact by forcing institutional officials to develop better security policies and practices. It is a timely and significant mandate that has created a heightened awareness of crime and security issues.

The Drug-Free Schools or Communities Act Amendments is also a welcomed and much needed federal mandate. Our colleges and universities should create opportunities for teaching responsibility and strong values. Effective alcohol and drug programming should be aimed at educating college students about their responsibility with regard to alcohol and drug abuse. The successful outcomes will be measured in reduced injuries and crime as well as better, more healthy citizens.

## ENDNOTES

1. Douglas F. Tuttle, *The Crime Awareness and Campus Security Act of 1990: Strategies for Compliance* (Hartford, Connecticut: International Association of Campus Law Enforcement Administrators, 1991), p. 1.

2. Federal Register, Vol. 55, No. 79, Tuesday, April 24, 1990, p. 4.

3. *FORUM, A Newsletter of the National Association of Student Personnel Administrators*, Washington, D.C. June/July, 1994 pp. 1 and 4.

4. Michael Clay Smith and Richard Fossey, *Crime On Campus: Legal Issues and Campus Administration* (Phoenix, Arizona: American Council On Educational Oryx Press, 1995), pp. 218 and 219.

5. *Complying With The Final Regulations:*, An advisory paper by the National Association of Student Personnel Administrators, Washington, D.C., August 1994, p. 3.

6. Ibid, pp. 7 and 8.

7. Smith and Fossey, p. 214.

8. Complying With the Final Regulations, p. 9.

9. Dennis Gregory, "Misguided Campaigns for the Release of Students' Disciplinary Records," *The Chronicle of Higher Education*, Vol. XL, Number 34, April 27, 1994, p. B1.

10. *Campus Crime*, (Silver Springs, Maryland: Business Publishers, Inc., 1995), February, 1995 Vol. 5, No. 2, p. 11.

11. *Donald D. Gehring*, "Disciplinary Records Remain Confidential Under FERPA," *NASPA Forum*, A Newsletter of the National Association of Student Personnel Administrators, Vol. 15, No. 6, March, 1995, p. 6.

12. *Campus Security Report*, (Port Washington, N.Y.: Rusting Publications, 1993), Vol. 5, No. 12, December 1993, p. 10 and 11.

# Chapter 10

# A COLLABORATIVE APPROACH

## INTRODUCTION

Achieving a reasonably safe campus environment is no easy task. Escalating crime problems, decreasing resources, public expectations, fundamental cultural differences, alcohol/drug abuse, and a campus community comprised of predominantly "post adolescent, pre-adults" all create special challenges for higher education administrators. The threats to a safe campus must be met with strong institutional commitments, effective programming, comprehensive security measures, and good personnel. However, when these operate and respond independently of each other the result is often incongruence in focus and ineffective crime prevention.

Perhaps the foundation to a comprehensive effort to create a safe campus is a collaborative approach. It should involve the participation of not only campus public safety officials but other campus constituencies in a formal, intentional collaborative framework. Such an approach offers a practical model for effectively dealing with campus crime and student misconduct in a comprehensive approach. It should involve student affairs officials, housing staff, police/security officials, student activities personnel, counselors, campus health care personnel, local law enforcement, and other community service agencies.

The collaborative approach rests on the concept that all campus officials as well as students should share the responsibility for creating a safe campus. No longer can the responsibility for crime prevention rest solely with the campus police/security director. In fact, some of the most effective deterrents to crime, violence, and misconduct can originate from the efforts of students and university officials who through effective policies and practices eliminate opportunities for criminal misconduct.

The most important aspect of the collaborative approach is the sharing of information, ideas, and problem-solving activities among participants. Regular meetings, formal communications, and reporting procedures should be implemented so that a proactive planning approach is employed rather than a reactive one. Good interpersonal relations among all campus personnel are important so that a clear understanding of the process and philosophy is established. There should be a unity between the campus police/security department and the institution as a whole. This can only be achieved and maintained with the ongoing participation of the decision-makers in all areas of campus activity. It is, however, very difficult to gain the participation of all the necessary players, often because each may lack some essential information and a grasp of the issues. Essentially, many campus crime prevention approaches are characterized by fragmentation and an "us and them" mentality. FIGURE 10-1 illustrates the variety of officials which are often involved when incidents occur.

There is an ancient African proverb which says: "It takes a whole village to raise a child." This proverb has timely implications for creating a safe campus. It compliments the philosophy of most institutions which promotes an holistic approach to student development. It calls for virtually every institutional member and every program to directly or indirectly enhance the academic, social, personal, and physical development of students. Issues of student misconduct and environmental safety are especially interwoven into this approach. A community-based approach is the premise for combating the threats to a tranquil campus and for effectively dealing with student misconduct. While not an all inclusive, the list of officials below represents some of the significant community or "village" members which should be active participants in a collaborative approach. Upon careful examination one can readily recognize that, at one time or another, each of these officials will be a participant in a campus-related issue involving college students and campus crime. Key officials in the collaborative approach include:

1. Dean of Students
2. Campus Police/Security
3. Student Activities Director
4. Student Development Officer
5. Student Health
6. Local Police
7. Local Court Officials
8. Housing/Residence Life Officials
9. Faculty
10. Counsellors
11. Athletic Officials
12. Student Government Association
13. Greek Organization Advisors
14. Campus Judicial Officials
15. Administrative Officials

The most serious error student affairs professionals, housing staffs, public safety officials, and other key players can make is to isolate

## Figure 10.1

## A COLLABORATIVE APPROACH TO DEALING WITH CRIME AND MISCONDUCT: A MODEL

## DEFINITIONS OF CATEGORIES

1. HOUSING RULES VIOLATIONS — Visitation policies, security breaches contraband possession, etc.

2. ALCOHOL/DRUG VIOLATIONS — Illegal possession, use, sale & distribution

3. CRIME/DISORDER AT OFF–CAMPUS ORGANIZATIONS — Any crime, noise complaints, disruptions, etc. at any student organization recognized by the institution.

4. CRIMINAL INCIDENTS ON CAMPUS — Murder, Rape, Robbery, Burglary, Assault, Theft, Vandalism, Disorderly Conduct, etc.

5. INSTITUTIONAL POLICY VIOLATION — Student Code of Conduct, Loitering, Abusive Language, Weapons Possession, etc.

6. MISCONDUCT AT SPECIAL EVENTS — Any crime, misbehavior, and/or rule violation at special events such as parties, concerts, athletic events, SGA sponsored activities, Greek activities etc.

7. CIVIL DISORDER — Large scale civil disobedience, building takeovers, riots, etc.

| MISCONDUCT | HOUSING | PUBLIC SAFETY | DISCIPLINE DEAN OF STUDENTS | STUDENT ACTIVITIES | COUNSEL-ING | HEALTH SERVICES | LOCAL POLICE |
|---|---|---|---|---|---|---|---|
| HOUSING | * | * | * | | * | * | |
| ALCOHOL/ DRUGS | * | * | * | * | * | * | * |
| CRIME/ DISORDER OFF CAMPUS ORGANIZA-IZATIONS | | * | | * | | | * |
| CRIMINAL INCIDENTS ON CAMPUS | * | * | * | | * | * | |

**Figure 10-1. Continued**

| MISCONDUCT | HOUSING | PUBLIC SAFETY | DISCIPLINE DEAN OF STUDENTS | STUDENT ACTIVITIES | COUNSEL-ING | HEALTH SERVICES | LOCAL POLICE |
|---|---|---|---|---|---|---|---|
| INSTITUTIONAL POLICIES | * | * | * | * | | | |
| MISCONDUCT AT SPECIAL EVENTS | | * | * | * | | | |
| CIVIL DISORDER | * | * | * | * | | * | |

themselves, thinking they are an independent entity. If programs, policies, and practices are to achieve success, these campus professionals will need to develop effective campus relationships as well as establish linkages with key community groups and officials. This process is an ongoing one that requires thoughtful planning and considerable skills. Proactive intervention must become the norm rather than the exception. It does not happen by accident but requires a commitment to a broad-based, collaborative approach. It requires that campus officials sustain their efforts through strong and meaningful processes, policies, and activities.

## RESPONDING TO THREATS: ON-CAMPUS COLLABORATIVE EFFORTS

The following sections will present several of the most common threats to a safe campus and offer sound practices designed for responding to these threats. These practices and models take critical elements for a safe campus presented in previous chapters of this book and describe how they work in unity through a collaborative approach. These team-based practices and strategies are not intended as exclusive recommended approaches, but they do offer model programs which, in one form or another, have been utilized effectively on other campuses. They are provided with the intention of generating ideas and stimulating further research for the development and implementation of similar programs designed for the unique needs of other campuses.

## VIOLENCE

Campus violence is a major threat to a safe campus community. Few campuses are immune from some acts of violence at one time or another.

As discussed earlier in this book, media reports of campus violence have increased and brought more attention to the problems associated with the issue. Murders, rapes, robberies, and assaults have reached epidemic proportions. Gun-related violence is becoming a menace on campuses across the nation.[1] In response to these circumstances, Congress responded with the Campus Security Act of 1990. Consequently, this federal mandate has forced college and university officials who were heretofore apathetic, to devote more attention and resources to the problem of campus violence. On some campuses, however, these efforts remain minimal at best and are typically fragmented. Often, the campus police/security force is the primary entity charged with responding to incidents of campus violence. Campus judicial officials may also deal with student perpetrators but may not be involved in the broader issue of cause and effect. Some small institutions rely largely on local police and/or contracted security guards to solve violence problems.

The good news is that many institutions have adopted proactive interaction strategies coupled with a team-based, collaborative approach. These programs bring together campus colleagues from several departments across campus to develop effective activities aimed at reducing violence-related problems. These measures bar or discourage students from bringing guns to campus or from resorting to violence, vigorously punish students for violent behavior, counsel students in conflict resolution, and develop programs which educate students about guns and violence.

## Guns and Violence: One University's Collaborative Approach
## A Scenario

During the late 1980s and early 1990s State University experienced a series of unrelated violent incidents on campus. Most of these incidents occurred in and around residence halls and involved both students and nonstudents. Guns were increasingly used in these incidents. On Monday night, December 16, 1991, a young man (nonstudent) was fatally shot in the head by another nonstudent while they were visiting some friends in a campus residence hall. The perpetrator was captured within minutes by campus police, incarcerated and eventually successfully prosecuted. Alcohol was determined to be a major factor in this incident. The incident sent shock waves throughout the campus community and around the state. It brought attention to the problems of violence at State University which had existed for several years. Media coverage was largely negative and created fear among students and parents. Newspaper articles like the one below stirred fears among many.

## DORM LIFE is wild at Weatherly

### Site of SU shooting no stranger to trouble

State University—To hear the students talk about it Weatherly Hall on most nights is a party dorm with an edge: blaring stereos, people running through the halls, plenty of drinking, lots of fights.

The State University dorm where a 21-year-old man was shot to death Sunday evening has had a tumultuous year. A few weeks ago, a student was charged with grazing five people when he shot a sawed-off shotgun on the back porch after a fight at a party.

And in the early morning following a September football game, a man shot a handgun outside Weatherly during a fight. No one was injured. Two Birmingham men were charged with disorderly conduct.

"This is the one where all the stuff happens," said Tim Spivey, a freshman, sitting outside Weatherly Monday afternoon. "I'll be trying to go to sleep and there'll be a firecracker going off in the hall and, automatically, I'll think someone's been shot."

Officials at State University had, in fact, been aware that gun possession, shooting incidents, and violence were becoming all too frequent. Campus police reports, discipline cases, and housing reports clearly indicated that assaults, harassment, and gun-related incidents were steadily on the rise. State University officials had previously discussed these issues and made some efforts toward reacting to individual incidents through housing policies, discipline, and police enforcement activities. However, these efforts were fragmented and lacked a comprehensive approach to the problems which vexed the campus community. In particular, these efforts failed to address the root causes of such lawlessness and offered no real solutions to their continued occurrences.

Following this deadly shooting, campus police student affairs officials, housing personnel, judicial officers, students, and others met to seriously address the issue of guns and violence at State University. What followed was perhaps a model for turning around a crime-ridden campus community to a more tranquil environment virtually threat-free.

First, an assessment was conducted to determine the extent of the problems. This process focused on: (1) Identifying the troublemakers; (2) Determining where these incidents typically occurred; (3) Determining when they occurred; (4) Analyzing the reason(s) or why they occurred; and (5) Identifying associated issues such as alcohol, drugs, security measure, etc. Second, a list of recommendations was developed aimed at both short and long-term solutions. This list is illustrated in Figure 10.2. Third, it was agreed upon by campus officials that a collaborative approach would best serve the needs of campus security and improved communications would be the foundation for such an approach. This involved improved monitoring of student behavior and criminal incidents. It called for better reporting and communications among campus officials. It included regular meetings to discuss and develop strategies. And finally, it initiated a planned response to crime, misconduct and crises.

**Figure 10.2**

**RECOMMENDATIONS REDUCING CAMPUS VIOLENCE AT STATE UNIVERSITY**

1. Increase physical security and access control in residence halls by removing outer door handles on all exterior doors except the main entrance.
2. Improve lighting in and around residence halls.
3. Place security monitors in residence halls to monitor access and perform security checks.
4. Improve enforcement of housing visitation policies and procedures.
5. Increase the number of campus police officers and specifically assign more officers to walking patrols in and around residential facilities, especially during nighttime hours.
6. Increase enforcement of university alcohol policies and violations of state and local alcohol laws.
7. Establish daily reporting procedures between police, housing, judicial affairs, student activities, athletics, and the vice president of student affairs. These reports include criminal incidents, misconduct, visitation violations, trespassing warnings, alcohol violations, and other occurrences.
8. Include students in developing strategies and plans for better campus security.
9. Strictly enforce violations of campus policies related to violence and weapons through extrication from housing, suspension from the institution, and expulsion.
10. Enforce through arrest and adjudication all acts of violence and weapons-related incidents.
11. Improve the scope and clarity of housing policies and procedures especially as they relate to behavior and security issues.
12. Under special circumstances and when appropriate upon legal advise, conduct inspections of residence halls to remove weapons.

Beginning immediately, these recommendations were gradually implemented throughout the spring semester of 1992. The results were phenomenal! In their first annual report following this incident, the campus police department reported a dramatic 21 percent drop in criminal incidents and a 24 percent reduction in arrests. Alcohol violations in residence halls and trespassing incidents also decreased. Following a tightening of security measures, the implementation of new procedures, and the adoption of a "zero-tolerance" approach to guns and violence on campus, living conditions in resident halls became pleasant and peaceful. Each year following these measures, incidents of violence and gun-related occurrences continued to decrease.

## RAPE

Rape on campus has received front-page coverage in daily newspapers and is a frequent topic on the TV talk show circuit. Research studies clearly indicate that rape, particularly acquaintance rape, is far more common on college campuses than once believed. Many contemporary university administrators are unsure just how serious the problem of rape on campus is, especially when charges of a near-epidemic appear to be contradicted by the low numbers of cases reported to campus police/ security agents. Further uncertainty exists about appropriate institution policies and procedures that colleges should install to reduce the likelihood of rape on campus.

Rape is generally defined in reform state statutes and in federal rape law as nonconsensual sexual penetration of an adolescent or adult obtained by physical force, by threat of bodily harm, or when the victim is incapable of giving consent by virtue of mental illness, mental retardation, or intoxication.[2]

While it is inconceivable that campus officials can ever prevent all rapes on campus, especially date rape, campus officials must develop effective strategies to educate college men and women about rape, provide assistance programming for victims, and to establish a meaningful plan for responding when rape does occur. A collaborative approach is the only effective way to address these concerns. The problem of rape calls for a broad-based participation in phases of rape prevention and response.

The two scenarios which follow offer descriptions of actual campus rape incidents (anonymously). One involves a stranger rape and the other a date rape. They illustrate the problem of campus rape.

## Two Campus Rape Scenarios

1. It was a warm November day in 1993 when Sharon strolled down the sidewalk of Small College on her way to the drugstore just off campus. As she passed by a church affiliated campus student center on the edge of campus, a seemingly friendly young man asked her to step inside to assist him with a chore. Since she had frequently visited this center, she complied with his request and went inside. There the man brutally raped her at gunpoint, tied her hands and feet with her undergarments, and warned her not to report him. Following an extensive investigation by campus police and two other law enforcement agencies, the suspect was never identified or apprehended. Sharon subsequently left school and returned home, permanently traumatized by the incident. While some efforts were made by campus officials to comfort and assist Sharon, there was no concerted approach in place to effectively deal with this circumstance. In fact, there was some reluctance by campus officials to formally address the incident since it occurred just off campus.

2. At about 10 P.M. on a Wednesday night in the spring of 1994, Teresa was visiting a male acquaintance in his athletic dorm room on the campus of Private University. After some brief conversation, the male friend initiated unwelcomed sexual advances toward Teresa. Despite her pleas to stop, the male student forced himself on Teresa and raped her. Ashamed, confused, and traumatized, Teresa did not immediately report the incident until the next morning. Following her physical examination with a physician and her voluntary statement to campus security, local police were advised. Ultimately, because it was "his word against hers," no charges were brought against the young man. Teresa appealed to campus judicial officials but met with less than enthusiastic support. The male perpetrator was a standout football player for the university.

## RESPONDING TO CAMPUS RAPE

These scenarios describe typical reports of rape that occur all too frequently on many campuses. What should college officials do? It is important to develop a rape prevention program to educate the campus community about rape, its potential, the risks, and the consequences. Teamwork is essential and should involve a wide variety of campus officials, students, and local agency support.

A primary component of a college's response to the rape issue is a carefully articulated policy against sexual assault, one that describes in concrete terms the behaviors that constitute rape, the avenues of reporting for any woman who is victimized, the entity within the university that will adjudicate alleged rapes, the possible sanctions that might occur, and the institution's stance on campus organizations where a violation occurs repeatedly. Effective dissemination of the policy involves such outlets as a direct letter to students from the president, admissions literature, new student-orientation, and the student newspaper.[3]

While campus rape stirs up pictures of dark-clothed strangers lurking in the shadows waiting to brutally rape college coeds, it is not the most common circumstance on college campuses. Acquaintance or date rape is by far the most frequent type of rape. Studies indicate that 80 percent of rape victims were acquainted with their assailant and over half (57 percent) of the rapes involved a date.[4] Therefore, it is important that campus officials address this issue and respond with effective strategies.

## PENN STATE BEHREND: A COLLABORATIVE APPROACH

Date rape programming at Penn State Erie, The Behrend College was developed in a proactive way and involves the team approach. Addressing both prevention and response, Penn State Behrend's philosophy is that a collaborative approach to this issue is the only way to effectively reach all students' needs. Prevention includes formal and informal presentations by campus police, health services, counseling services, and residential life staff. Response includes a step-by-step procedure for assisting rape victims from medical treatment to advocacy during legal action, and the application campus departments have teamed with community social service agencies like Rape Crises.

### Prevention

The campus police department at Penn State Behrend uses a series of handouts about date rapes and utilizes information tables in the student union building to disseminate them and respond to questions from students. These handouts are also used at formal presentations given by campus police officers and crime prevention specialists.

The campus health services staff established a women's health clinic which includes intensive information about women's health issues. These clinics are ongoing and include physical exams and education sessions on date rape.

The Penn State Behrend's counseling services operates a "one-on-one" program to assist in the prevention of date rape. This program is usually provided as a part of the counseling process when students seek assistance with domestic problems such as abuse.

The residence life staff at Penn State Behrend developed a unique program called "Creative Dating." This provides for open discussion on issues of sex, dating, relationships, and date rape.

These efforts are examples of the teamwork approach date rape prevention. There is a constant networking between these departments. An ongoing evaluation of these programs helps officials refine strategies and develop new ideas.

### Response

When date rape cannot be prevented, the response process is activated at Penn State Behrend. The response process for date rape is established to assure the victim that her welfare is top priority. The "Guide For Sexual Assault Victims" was developed by the health services staff to assist date rape victims. It provides a step-by-step approach to the problem including information on medical treatment, emotion support, legal services, and victim advocacy.

Collaboration between campus officials and the local rape crisis center assists the victim from the minute the rape is reported and throughout the counseling process. The assigned counselor will actually accompany the victim during every phase of the process. Family support counseling is also available. On campus counseling services also works closely with the victim and is available throughout the process.

Campus police officers are also trained in the handling of rape victims and they stress that the victim's safety and welfare are first priorities. Campus police will process reports of rape and assist in the prosecution of offenders if the victim is willing to pursue prosecution. The campus police will conduct appropriate investigations, take statements, process evidence, and work with local authorities to ensure proper adjudication. They will also provide appropriate information to Penn State Behrend judicial officials for possible disciplinary actions.

Discipline sanctions is still another avenue the victim may consider. Once identified, a student suspect can be charged with the appropriate violation under the student conduct standards. The campus judicial process allows for several options for adjudicating the alleged violation through the university's student judicial system.[5]

This collaborative approach found at Penn State Behrend is but one example of such team efforts at colleges and universities. It is by no means all-encompassing but presents the basic components of a response to the threat of date rape on campus.

## AN INNOVATIVE APPROACH

Michigan State University has created a novel approach to responding to rape and sexual assault. This innovative idea embraces the collaborative approach through its development, dissemination, and implementation. The Department of Public Safety at MSU developed the "DPS Sexual Assault Guarantee" aimed at assisting victims of rape and sexual assault.[6] The purpose in developing this written guarantee has four objectives as follows:

1. Stimulate awareness, discussion, and reporting of the "hidden" and often unreported crime of acquaintance rape.
2. Help put sexual assault victims more at ease in accessing and working with their local police officers.
3. Emphasize a strong organizational commitment by the Department of Public Safety (DPS) to sexual assault victims.
4. Enable DPS to reach out to sexual assault victims, who have already suffered much trauma, to provide help so that they are not further victimized by the criminal justice system itself.

The "DPS Sexual Assault Guarantee" is widely distributed throughout the Michigan State University campus community. Copies are given to parents and presented during summer parent orientation programs. Thousands of copies have been disseminated to students and student organizations at the beginning of each fall semester. Large posters are printed and displayed across campus, particularly in residence halls.

As mentioned, this is a collaborative effort. A draft of this document was submitted to groups throughout the campus community. The final product was one which was thoroughly discussed and refined by a wide cross-section of the MSU community. The "DPS Sexual Assault Guarantee" is presented in Figure 10-3.

## CAMPUS DISRUPTION AND CRISIS

Contemporary university administrators recognize that their campuses are threatened, to some extent, by crime. Most of these officials readily agree that campus police and security measures are important in preventing crime and misconduct. They understand the implications of negligence, foreseeability, and liability issues. Crisis preparedness is also a concern to administrators. They take extensive steps to develop crisis

**Figure 10.3**

## DPS SEXUAL ASSAULT GUARANTEE

Sexual assaults, including date/acquaintance rape, are a very serious concern of DPS. If you feel you are the victim of a sexual assault on campus, your department of Public Safety will guarantee you the following:

1. We will meet with you privately, at a place of your choice in this area, to take a complaint report.
2. We will not release your name to the public or to the press.
3. Our officers will not prejudice you, and you will not be blamed for what occurred.
4. We will treat you and your particular case with courtesy, sensitivity, dignity, understanding, and professionalism.
5. If you feel more comfortable talking with a female or male officer, we will do our best to accommodate your request.
6. We will assist you in arranging for any hospital treatment or other medical needs.
7. We will assist you in privately contacting counseling, safety, advising, and other available resources.
8. We will fully investigate your case, and will help you to achieve the best outcome. This may involve the arrest and full prosecution of the suspect responsible. You will be kept up-to-date on the progress of the investigation and/or prosecution.
9. We will continue to be available for you, to answer your questions, to explain the systems and processes involved (prosecutor, courts, etc.), and to be a listening ear if you wish.
10. We will consider your case seriously regardless of your gender or the gender of the suspect.

If you feel you are a sexual assault victim, call your Department of Public Safety at 355-2221, and say you want to privately make a sexual assault complaint. You may call any time of day or night.

If we fail to achieve any part of the above guarantee, the Director of Public Safety, Dr. Bruce Benson (355-2223), will meet with you personally to address any problems. DPS wants to make the MSU campus safe for students, faculty, staff, and visitors.

management plans which are aimed at natural disasters, explosions, fire, and other potential disasters. However, few institutions of higher learning are adequately prepared to deal with civil unrest and unexpected disruptions which create serious threats to lives and property. The well-developed emergency plans of the 1960s and 70s which were geared for student protests, sit-ins, and similar social demonstrations have now gathered nearly three decades of dust. Typically, these sorts of planned protests were somewhat easily anticipated. Today's threats of large-scale disruptions may be spontaneous, unorganized, and deadly.

Increasingly, campus public safety officials are faced with a new type of crisis. Often associated with special events such as rock concerts, step shows, athletic events and parties, these disruptions and disorders create havoc for colleges and universities. Unlike the protests of the 1960s, guns and other weapons are frequently involved in today's campus disruptions. Large-scale random violence and lawlessness often mock these crises.

When these crises occur on campus, the world treats them differently from the way it treats such events when they occur off campus—whether or not they involve students. Campus crises are looked at, rightly or wrongly, as the institution's problem, or even its fault. Media coverage is often aimed at discrediting the institution and may transform facts into inflammatory issues.

What defines a crisis may be all, more than, or a part of the following: the nature of the event; how many and how quickly people need help, informed, or both; who and how many need interpretation of the events; how assessable those people are; how much interaction with the media is necessary; what the media chooses to emphasize; who and how many people need emergency care; how much the institution needs to assert control and demonstrate that it is capable of responding; and how quickly the institution needs to respond. Crisis may also be defined by feelings of panic, fear, danger, or shock. Each crisis is unique, and although many institutions have established crisis management process, administrators adjust and respond differently to each situation.[7]

The following scenario describes a real-life incident that occurred on the campus of Jacksonville State University (JSU) in 1989. Nothing even similar had ever occurred at JSU and no one anticipated it would ever happen. Officials there were unprepared to deal with the incident and the reverberations which followed. This scenario will be followed by JSU's response and its preparation for future critical situations. The intent of this format is to offer a suggestion for other institutions which may not be prepared for unexpected crises.

## The Scenario

## CIVIL DISTURBANCE INCIDENT
## JACKSONVILLE STATE UNIVERSITY
### April 18, 1989

On Tuesday night, April 18 the Alpha Phi Alpha fraternity sponsored a Step Show in the Theron Montgomery Building Auditorium. Approximately 400 students were present. During this event several members of another fraternity, Kappa Alpha Psi, came into the Auditorium to disrupt the Step Show. At approximately 9:50 P.M. a fight broke out between members of these two fraternities. Two University police officers who were providing security for the event were successful in stopping the fight. Several other on-duty University police officers were summoned to assist. At approximately 10:25 P.M. another more violent altercation occurred between members of these fraternities including chairs being thrown. The four police officers who were still present were unable to separate those involved and to regain control. At approximately 10:27 P.M. a call for police back-up went out and other officers arrived within minutes. In trying to control the fighting and disperse the crowd at least two officers were assaulted by students. One student was arrested in the auditorium. The University Police supervisor in charge closed the party and the students gathered just outside the Auditorium on Trustee Circle where further threats and disorderly conduct continued.

At approximately 10:35 P.M. JSU's Director of Public Safety arrived on the scene and assumed control. He directed police officers to disperse the crowd. The director and officers instructed the students to disperse and return to their residence halls. The students were reluctant to disperse but slowly moved toward Daugette Hall. Profanities, verbal abuse, and threats were then directed at police officers. During this time one student who struck an officer was arrested just outside the Theron Montgomery Building.

By this time officers from the Jacksonville Police Department and Calhoun County Sheriff's Department had arrived to assist. As the crowd moved in the area of Fitzpatrick and Weatherly Halls a Sheriff's Deputy was struck in the head by a rock and other items were thrown at police officers. At this point in time a 10-00 call (urgent, officer needs help) went out from the Jacksonville Police Department. Several other police agencies responded which brought the number of police officers to an estimated forty-five (45) officers.

The crowd (now near an estimated 550) became increasingly hostile and abusive toward police officers. Four more students were arrested on charges ranging from disorderly conduct to assault and resisting arrest. Several University Police officers were injured. With the situation becoming more volatile, the Director of Public Safety made the decision to organize the police officers into several squads in an effort to move students into nearby residence halls. This was done at approximately 11:20 A.M. and was successful in bringing an end to the crisis.

The Deputy received a laceration to the head and required several stitches. A University police officer who was taken to the Jacksonville Emergency Room sustained a fractured shoulder. Several other campus officers received minor injuries. One student, who was arrested, was taken to the Jacksonville Emergency Room where he was treated and released, receiving several stitches in his head. One student was reportedly injured in an altercation in the Montgomery Building but has not been identified.

During the disruption a Sheriff's Deputy, without proper authority, called for a Jacksonville Fire Truck. Fire Department personnel did not assist in any way nor were hoses ever removed from the truck. While one agency made available tear gas, its use was never considered. Shotguns were displayed by officers from other police agencies. Control of outside agency personnel was a concern.

This incident created wide media coverage in all forms — newspapers, radio, and television. By and large, the slant was a negative one. The element of white police officers and black students played well for journalists. The repercussions were felt locally, state-wide, and nationally as parents, human rights organizations, and police critics seized the opportunity to further incite angry sentiments. Some students who were interviewed described incidents of police brutality and racism despite the fact that they were neither eyewitnesses nor present at the event! Recovery from this onslaught of criticism and "Monday morning quarterbacking" was long and hard for university officials.

## A RESPONSE TO CAMPUS DISRUPTIONS

Officials at Jacksonville State University responded in both reactive and proactive ways. The first reactive task at hand was to assess the damages and make determinations as to cause and effect. Several assessment/investigatory processes were initiated simultaneously. The president of the University immediately met with the director of public safety, vice president for student affairs, dean of students, director of student activities, news information coordinator, and other key officials to conduct what he labeled a "post mortem" of the entire episode of April 18. From that meeting it was decided to initiate several assessment efforts to determine the facts and to make recommendations for possible disciplinary actions for students and employees.

The University Police Department conducted its own internal investigation. This involved taking sworn statements from all officers on duty on the night of April 18. It also involved the questioning of student participants and local public safety officials who responded. Evidence such as the city police audio recording of radio and telephone traffic was also obtained to develop a time line and to corroborate statements. This report was sent to the vice president of student affairs and then on to the president.

The president appointed a diverse investigative committee to assess all aspects of the incident and to submit its findings and recommendations. This committee was comprised of faculty members, administrative officials, police officers, and local government officials. It was a representative group in terms of race, gender, and position in the institution. The final report from this committee was submitted to the president of the university.

The Division of Student Affairs also conducted an assessment of the scheduled event, assigned responsibilities, fraternity-related issues, student participation, campus police role, and facility concerns. The vice president for student affairs, dean of students, director of student activities, and director of public safety each gathering pertinent information and compiled a comprehensive findings report.

It is interesting that all of these assessment findings paralleled each other. Essentially, they reported that it was nonstudents who precipitated the violence, not JSU fraternity members. Further, the findings of these committees and officials were that the actions of one single police officer resulted in students' complaints of excessive force and racism. This officer's employment with the University was subsequently terminated following proper procedures. The findings concluded that generally the police decisions and actions were appropriate under these exigent conditions. Civil disobedience, violence, and disorderly conduct were among the violations committed by a number of students. Several students were suspended from the University.

Recommendations emanating from these assessment efforts included: better special events security; collaborative planning for events; improved police-community communication; cultural diversity-sensitivity training; and better screening of police applicants.

These recommendations became the basis for further proactive measures which would be implemented by university officials. As listed below, these programs and processes significantly enhanced police-community relations and improved conditions for future special events.

### Proactive Measures

1. A campus crisis/disorder planning seminar was hosted by JSU and attended by student affairs officials, law enforcement officers, members of the media,

and others around the state. Critical elements of a crisis, basic planning principles, and response measures were the focus of this seminar.

2. The University Police Department developed an Emergency Response Plan for dealing with campus disorders and disasters.

3. An Administrative Response Team was organized to be activated in the event of any major campus crisis and to serve as a coordinating/advisory group. This team consists of the following officials:

   Director of Student Activities
   Director of Campus News Information
   Director of Health Services
   Director of Housing
   Dean of Students
   Vice President for Student Affairs
   Director of Physical Plant
   Director of Public Safety

4. Cultural sensitivity training and use of force training was included as part of the required annual training for campus police personnel.

5. Mutual assistance procedures with local law enforcement and other public safety agencies were clarified and improved.

6. Additional minority campus police officers were hired and a commitment to maintain an acceptable level of diversity was affirmed.

7. Meetings were held with student leaders and student organizations to discuss problems, issues, and solutions for special events.

8. A student-initiative to employ additional security at special events was adopted.

9. Enhanced security measures for special events were proposed by students and adopted for implementation. These included improved I.D. checks, use of metal detectors, guest lists, and required adult supervision.

10. Improved collaborative efforts were implemented among student affairs staff and other campus constituencies which included meetings to discuss issues and problems, formal reports, clear patterns of communication among campus officials, and ongoing assessment strategies.

## A COLLABORATIVE COMMUNICATIONS MODEL

Collaborative efforts and processes may be both formal and informal. Many higher education institutions, because of their collegial environment, naturally develop collaborative approaches to a host of circumstances. Creating a safe campus and responding to occasional threats requires that university officials develop definitive processes which offer clarity of role and responsibility. These processes should delineate communications modes and patterns. In the event of any threat to a safe campus, whether it be student misconduct, rape, violence, or a major crisis—every key organization member should understand that a holistic, collaborative approach will best serve the institution. In developing proactive strategies the "left hand must know what the right hand is doing." Coordination and cooperation will result in better outcomes. Student affairs, housing, campus police, student health services, student activities, judicial affairs, and other campus constituencies are all critical elements which must be tied together in a collaborative communications framework. Figure 10-4 illustrates such a collaborative communications model.

**Figure 10.4**

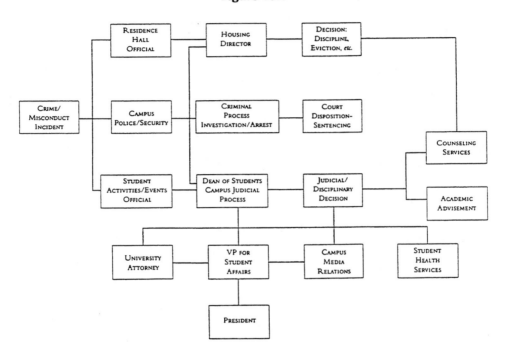

## SUMMARY

It is foreseeable that some type of crime, emergency, misconduct, and/or crisis will occur on most college and university campuses. While proactive collaborative planning can reduce the risks associated with these incidents, preparedness for an effective response is essential. Heretofore, campus officials were often devoted little effort developing strategies which brought a broad cross section of key officials together in the process. Consequently, critical incidents often create havoc and bring negative attention to the institution.

Collaborative approaches for a wide variety of potential threats to a safe campus may take on many different forms. Each institution should design these approaches to meet their unique organizational configurations and special circumstances. Communication among colleagues and key university officials is a key to effective collaboration. Formal patterns of monitoring, reporting, and planning should be developed and clearly articulated to all campus participants. Informal relationships and dialogue should become a routine organizational practice.

Crime, violence, and other threats to a safe campus can no longer be the exclusive responsibility of the campus police and security department. The proverb "It takes a whole village to raise a child" is particularly applicable to the collaborative model. Campus administrators and officials should adopt a collegial, cooperative approach to creating a safe campus. Students need to know that every office on campus is connected to every other office in a concerted effort to provide a safe living and learning environment and to respond to their needs when threats occur. Creating a safe campus is a shared responsibility, bringing together all critical components into one comprehensive effort.

## ENDNOTES

1. Douglas Lederman, "Weapons On Campus?", *The Chronicle of Higher Education*, Vol. XI, No. 27, March 9, 1994, pp. A33 & A 34.
2. Mary Koss, "Rape On Campus: Facts and Measures," *Planning For Higher Education*, Volume 20, Spring 1992, p. 21.
3. Ibid, p. 25.
4. Ibid, p. 23.
5. Todd C. Allen, "Date Rape Programming at Penn State Behrend," *Campus Law Enforcement Journal*, Vol. 20, No. 3, May–June, 1990 pp. 13–15.
6. Bruce L. Benson, "The Public Safety "Sexual Assault Guarantee" at Michigan State University", *Campus Law Enforcement Journal*, Vol. 27, No. 6, Nov.–Dec. 1992, pp. 26–28.
7. Dorothy Siegel, *Campuses Respond To Violent Tragedy*, (Phoenix, Arizona: American Council On Education and Oryx, Press, 1996), p. 250.

# INDEX

## A

Academia as big business, 12
Alcohol or drug use, impact on incidence of crime, 9, 31–38, 41, 43, 85, 94, 103, 110
Association of Student Judicial Affairs, 27
Atlanta (GA) Journal-Constitution's report on campus incidents of violence, 30

## B

Bates College, 137
Bethune-Cookman College, 29
Birmingham-Southern College, 130

## C

Campus crime, 9, 14–17, 19, 27–29, 31–36, 38, 39, 41–43, 85, 94, 101, 104, 109–112, 132, 133, 141, 144, 156–170
  alcohol and drug abuse, 9, 31, 36–38, 43, 85, 94, 103, 104, 110, 141
    implication in sexual disease and violence, 37–38, 141
    implication in disorderly conduct, 38, 41, 85, 94, 104, 110
  assaults, 9, 17, 31, 109
    aggravated incidents, 31, 144
  bicycle thefts, 43
  burglaries, 9, 42, 144
  carjackings, 9, 17
  fights, 38, 106, 107, 119, 145
  firearms and guns, 9, 16, 27–29, 109, 157–160
    drive-by shootings on campus, 29
    epidemic of gun-related violence, 28
    leading cause of African-American deaths, 28

    second leading cause of teenage deaths, 28
  harassment, 9, 31, 32
    homosexuals, 32
    racial/ethnic minorities, 32, 94
    reverse harassment, 33
    sexual, 31
  hate crimes, 9, 32, 43–44
  hazing, 9, 33–34, 38
    definition, 33
    liabilities, 34
  homicides, 14, 17, 19, 144
  myths and realities, 14–17
  personal violence, 16, 19, 31
  property crimes, 16, 42, 94, 101, 132
    bicycle thefts, 43, 132
    burglaries, 9, 42
    motor vehicle thefts, 9, 17, 42, 43, 144
    racial tensions, 9, 14, 32–33, 41, 94
  rapes, 9, 14, 16, 17, 19, 34–36, 38, 39, 109–110, 141, 144, 160–165
    date rape, 35, 38, 109, 162–165; Stanford survey results, 35
    gang rape, 38
  records, reporting, and disclosure, 13, 15, 32, 35, 42
  robberies, 9, 144
  sexual offenses other than rape, 35
  shootings, 9, 16, 17, 27–29, 39, 156–160
  stalkings, 32
  safety and security assessments, 9, 10, 27
  student perpetrators and victims, 15, 16, 42
  telephone harassment, 32, 35
  theft, 39, 111, 132, 133, 144
  vandalism, 32, 43
  zero-tolerance approach, 11, 17, 112, 160
Campus environment (*see also* Physical and environmental security)

Campus environment (*Continued*)
  administration leadership, 14, 112–117, 124
    direct support to all related campus
      constituencies, 17
    firearms ban, 29, 39
    institutional policy statements on crime
      and violence, 17, 112
    justice to be served commitment, 71
    policy against sexual assault, 161–165
    security goals, objectives, assessments,
      and programs, 9, 17, 112–117
    zero-tolerance approach to crime, 11, 17,
      112, 160
  athletic events, 9, 29, 31, 40–41
  collaborative approach to ensuring a safe
    campus, 153–172
    communications model, 170–171
    information sharing, 153
    key officials identification, 154–156, 171
  mirrors of national agenda, social health,
    wealth, and crime, 3, 16, 17, 25, 27,
    40, 83, 85, 86, 103
  social activities, 9, 29, 31, 40–41
  student misconduct and disorder, 4–7,
    40–42, 104, 111, 164–170
  vehicular traffic, 7, 39, 130
  violence, 9, 16, 17, 28, 30, 31, 37–38, 112,
    141, 156–160
Campus housing, 9, 19, 31, 32, 94–96, 103–121
  accessibility, 9, 38–39, 113, 116, 124
    security options to control access to
      residences, 116–117
  institutional liability, 20–21, 34, 104, 113,
    119, 124, 142
  nonstudent intruders, 38–39, 43, 113, 124
  off-campus residences, 19, 49, 107, 119, 121
    fraternity and sorority houses, 107, 119,
      145
    housing units located near campus but
      not owned by institution, 107, 119
    apartment safety inspection
      programs, 120
    security standards, 120
    housing units owned and operated by
      institution, 107, 119
  on-campus residences, 18–19, 105–107, 121
    apartments, 101, 106
    fraternity and sorority houses, 106, 145
    residence halls/dormitories, 9, 19, 31,
      32, 94–96, 101, 105

    apartment-like setting in dorms, 105
    coeducational dorms, 104
    cultural preference settings, 105
    relaxation of institutional discipli-
      nary rules, 39, 104
  security considerations and susceptibil-
    ity to crime, 105–109, 113–119
  student leadership, management, and
    shared responsibility, 108, 117, 121
  crime prevention and security
    enhancement programs, 118–119,
    121
  vulnerability to crime, post-adolescent lack
    of sense to, 19, 108, 112, 117, 121
Campus police (*see* Police and security
  services)
Campus Security Act reporting requirements,
  13, 15, 22, 42, 141, 143–147, 157
Chronicle of Higher Education, 25, 27
Columbia University, 6, 37
Community-based policing, 76–77, 80–81,
  83–101, 125, 153–172
  "Adopt-A-Cop," 98
  campus housing safety strategies, 9, 19, 31,
    32, 94–99
  characteristics and principles, 88
  citizen involved crime prevention
    strategies, 94
  collaborative approach, identification of
    key officials, 154–156
  comprehensive crime analysis in criminal
    incidents, 93
  cross-cultural communication skills, 91
  evaluations by public surveys, 92
  evaluations by key student groups, 93
  historic overview of concept evolution,
    84–87
  mission statement, 87, 92
  partnership and problem solving, 88, 91,
    99–101, 154
  patrol methods and factors, 97–98
  performance-based reward motivators, 91
  personnel characteristics for successful
    community policing, 90
  preventive patrol of traditional policing,
    94
  proactive, decentralized, empowerment-
    based philosophy, 87–89
  San Francisco Police Department func-
    tioning as social services agency, 85

Community-based policing (*Continued*)
  security escorts, 98
  team policing for neighborhoods, 85
  ten principles of community policing, 88
  University of South Florida implementa-
    tion of community policing, 89–90
Cornell University, 105
*Crime at College: The Student Guide to Personal
  Safety,* 24

**D**

Drug-Free Schools and Communities Act, 38,
  141–143
Duke University, 39, 136

**E**

Evergreen State College, 33

**F**

Florida State University, 73
Free Speech Movement, 6

**H**

Harvard School of Public Health, 28, 43, 110
Higher education institutions, 3–25
  influences of economic change, 5, 12
    declining enrollments due to percep-
      tions of threat, 13, 29
    decreasing students vs. increasing num-
      ber of colleges, 12
    discounted tuition, 8
    endowments, 3, 5, 12
    enrollments, 3, 7
      inducements, 18
      minority students, 7
      on-line admissions, 7
      recruiting programs, 12, 18
      retention programs, 18, 19
    federal program funding, 3, 5
    fundraising, 12
    graduate fellowships, 5
    grant writing, 12
    image making, 18, 121
    philanthropic contributions, 3, 14
    rate of inflation, 8
    student loans, 5
    subsidies, 5

    tax initiatives, 8
  influences of social/political change, 5
    civil rights movement, 5, 6, 40, 85
    drug use, 5
    federal funding, 5
    G.I. Bill, 5, 51
    1990's societal change factors, 8
    population diversity, 7, 49
    undergraduate students as primary
      customers, 8
    selective service system, 5, 6
    sports programs, 9
    student activism, 6, 40–42, 85–87
      demonstrations, 42, 85–87
      direct confrontation tactics, 6
      intentional lawbreaking, 6
      misconduct and disorder, 4–7, 40–42,
        104, 111, 164–170
      sit-ins and protests, 7, 85, 86
      university policies and officials, 6
      Vietnam War, 5, 6, 40, 85–87

**I**

Institutional liability and relationship
  theories, 6, 20–21, 34, 113, 129, 142
  *in loco parentis,* 6, 20, 104
  landlord-tenant, 20, 63, 104, 113
  landowner-business invitee, 20
  sexual aggression offenses and liability, 36,
    142
  student-institution, 104
  welfare and safety obligation, 20
*Involving Colleges,* George Kuh, John Schuh,
  Elizabeth Whitt

**J**

Jacksonville State University, 28, 39, 40, 54,
  93, 109, 136, 166–170
Johns Hopkins University, 12

**K**

Kansas State University, 21
Kent State University, 6, 28

**L**

Lehigh University, 13, 71, 113
Likins, Peter, 71

**M**

Marijuana (*see* Alcohol and drug abuse)
Marquette University, 108
Massachusetts Institute of Technology, 43
Michigan State University, 164
Mississippi State University, 53
Mount Holyoke, 58

**O**

Oklahoma City University, 39
Olivet College, 41

**P**

Peel, Sir Robert, 84
Penn State Behrend, 162–163
Physical and environmental security, 124–138
    campus access, nonstudent, 124, 125, 130
        open or closed campus, 125
    community-based policing, 125, 127, 132
    defensible space theories, 126
    security policies, designation of office
        responsible for maintaining plans
        and documents, 125, 128
    security strategies for physical spaces,
        129–137
        facility access, 132–134
            areas most vulnerable to criminal
                behavior, 133
            electronic security system, 132
            wireless detection system to deter
                theft, 133
        grounds and landscaping, 135
        lighting and illumination standards,
            outdoor, 134
        neighborhood adjacency, 131–132
        parking areas, 136–137
            audio and visual closed-circuit TV
                surveillance, 137
            emergency call boxes, 137
            lighting, high-mast, reflector style
                illumination, 136
        perimeter, 129–131
            surveillance cameras, 130
            vehicular access, 7, 39, 130
    security vulnerability assessment audit,
        127–128

Pine Manor College, 21
Police and security services, 7, 10, 66–81
    campus police recruited from retired law
        enforcement personnel, 68
    community-based policing, 76–77, 80–81,
        83–101, 125
    degree holding security administrators,
        emphasis on, 69
        organizational reporting to vice presi-
            dents of student affairs, 69, 71
    law enforcement role, 72–74, 77–78
    liability applications for security viola-
        tions, 70, 113, 142
        breach of contract theory based on
            assurance of safety protection,
            70–71
        negligence theory based on tort law,
            70–71
    public safety department leadership, 74–77
        empowerment models, 76
        military model and authority-based
            values, 75–77
    rape response processes, 163–164
    recommendations to clarify police role
        authority, 74
    responsibilities and services, 77–80
        crime prevention, 79
        facilities security, 78, 125
        fire safety, 79
        parking management, 79
        school maintenance staff, evolution
            from, 66–67, 71
        special event security, 78, 124, 169–170
        special services provided by campus
            police, 80
    service role, 72–74, 78–80
    watchman or guard, evolution from, 67–68
    University of Maryland establishment of
        safety/security departments, 68
    Yale Campus Police establishment, 67

**R**

Rape, 9, 14, 16, 17, 19, 34, 38, 39, 109–110, 141,
    144, 160–165
Records, reporting, and disclosure, 13, 15, 32,
    35, 42, 140–151
    Campus Security Act, 141, 143–147, 151,
        157

Records, reporting, disclosure (*Continued*)
  annual security policy report informa-
    tion points, 145–146
  annual sexual offense prevention
    policy report information points,
    146–147
  definition of campus via federal
    regulations, 144
  public's right to know about campus
    crime, 144, 147
  Drug-Free Schools and Communities Act
    Amendments, 141–143, 151
  alcohol or drug use, impact on inci-
    dence of crime, 9, 31–38, 41, 43,
    85, 94, 103, 110, 141–143
  standards of conduct communique to
    students, 142
  substance abuse prevention programs
    assessment, 143
  Family Rights and Privacy Act, 148–150
    student information disclosure regu-
      lations, 148–150
  student disciplinary or crime records,
    147–151
  student-perpetuated acts of violence, 140
  Syracuse University's disclosure and
    reporting recommendations for
    crime-related incidents, 150
Rice University, 30
Rutgers University, 41, 109

**S**

Simon's Rock College, 28
Southeast Missouri State University, 30
Southern Illinois University, 37
Stanford University, 58
Stetson University, 107
Student affairs leadership role, 48–64
  appointment of chief student affairs officer,
    30
  cultural and ethnic diversity, 49
  dean of students origination, 51
  development of intellectual and educa-
    tional processes, 52
  mission statement, organizational design,
    and specific goals, 53–57
  off-campus residences, 49
  out-of-class experiences, 48, 49

organizational reporting of police to vice
  president of student affairs, 71
orientation activities, 48
peer influences, 48
policies and practices to ensure campus
  safety, 57–64
  prospective student letter, 58
  orientation activities, 58
  student conduct codes, written, 58–61
    academic honor codes, 59
    adjudication of conduct code
      violations, 61–63
    due process rights in public versus
      private academic institutions,
      62
    campus judicial system bias toward
      protection of academic
      community, 62
    criminal judicial system bias toward
      protection of the accused
      rights, 62
    disciplinary codes, 59
    viability strategies for austere
      economies, 53
  security issues role, 48
  undergraduate age, 49
  "whole person" education role, 51, 52, 64
Swarthmore College, 32
Syracuse University, 150

**T**

Towson State University, 16, 37, 39, 109
  alcohol and drug use survey results, 37
Tufts University, 43

**U**

University of Alabama, 42
University of Arkansas, 39
University of California—Berkeley, 6
University of California—Riverside, 30
University of Florida, 108, 120
University of Maryland, 68
University of Minnesota, 137
University of Notre Dame, 132
University of South Florida, 89
University of Tennessee, 29
University of Wisconsin, 42

University-community relations, 21–25, 131
    characteristics of student-community
        coexistence, 22–23
    disclosure of student organizations' off-
        campus criminal incidents, 22
    fraternities, 23, 30, 38, 40–41, 106, 145
    jurisdiction/responsibility issues, 23
    newspaper advertisement relative to frater-
        nity behaviors, 23
    off-campus crime, 24
    social-environmental assumptions, 131
Uniform Crime Reporting System, 15, 16, 28,
    31, 43, 44

**V**

Vanderbilt University, 131
Violence, collaborative measures to contradict,
    156–160
    State University recommendations to
        reduce campus violence, 159
Violent Crime Control and Law Enforcement
    Act, 30
*Violent Crimes and Other Forms of Victimization
    in Residence Halls,* Carolyn J. Palmers,
    112

**Y**

Yale University, 67